THE ART
OF THE
WOODCARVER

The best from **WOODCarving** *magazine*

GUILD OF MASTER CRAFTSMAN PUBLICATIONS LTD

This collection first published in 1996 by
Guild of Master Craftsman Publications Ltd,
Castle Place, 166 High Street, Lewes,
East Sussex BN7 1XU

ISBN 1 86108 011 5

Printed and bound in Great Britain by
the University Press, Cambridge

Front cover photograph supplied by Ray Winder

Back cover photograph supplied by Stan Kimm

CONTENTS

NOTES

PLEASE NOTE that names, addresses, prices, circumstances etc, which were correct at the time the articles were originally published, may since have changed.

INTRODUCTION

WOODCARVING is an ancient craft, probably the oldest known to man, and until recently it was a familiar craft. Not so very long ago, it was quite common for domestic woodwork to be decorated with carving of one sort or another.

Unfortunately, by the 1930s a decorative style had developed that didn't require carved wood. Increasing mechanisation in woodworking led to more simple, machine-made decoration – simple mouldings can be produced on machines at a rate of hundreds of metres a day, whereas a craftsman could take days completing complex carved mouldings. Nowadays, except in a few cases, industrial production avoids the use of intricate woodcarvings.

The demand for antique furniture, however, has been responsible for the preservation of many carving skills – only a woodcarver can repair woodcarvings, of course. Furniture restoration workshops around the country have been the mainstay of woodcarving for the latter half of this century.

But woodcarving is now undergoing a revival, as many people begin to discover the pleasures and potential of carved wood. Power tools have been developed to speed production, and copy carving machines can mass produce some forms of work, although to get the full range of shapes possible, carvers still have to resort to hand tools, be they chisels, punches or abrasive riffler rasps.

Craftsmen with years of technical expertise are handing on their skills to artists with highly imaginative ideas, and woodcarving has also become a popular hobby. The result is a healthy and growing body of creative woodcarving.

The articles in this book have been selected from the pages of *Woodcarving* magazine to show the diversity of modern woodcarving. This ancient craft is being used in more ways now than ever before: from monumental works to netsuke, from lifelike precision to unrestrained abstract sculpture.

I hope that the diversity of work in this book will astonish and inspire readers to find out more about the developing craft and art of woodcarving.

Neil Bell, Editorial Manager.

Arc by Bev Houlding
This is the latest of a series of screens based on figures climbing in and out of shapes, contrasting the rough and dull with the smooth and shiny. Intrigued by naturally-worn surfaces, the textures within the carefull, carved shapes are worked freely, leaving much to chance

Creek Pool by Bev Houlding
Bev's images are very structural. The design is carefully drawn onto the primed MDF before painting. The carved and machine-routed lines allow a free range of paint experimentation — going 'over the line' is no problem; a quick wipe of excess paint, and the line reappears

CARVED

In the hands of Bev and Mark Houlding,

ollowing college (Bev BED, Goldsmiths — Mar
MA, Royal College of Art) Bev and Mar
Houlding taught in London schools an
colleges. This provided them with regula
incomes but, inevitably, left little energy fc
artistic inspiration at the end of the day.

The situation changed dramatically in 1984 whe
they met, married and established Screens Gallery, i
Emsworth, Hampshire. They found they had a mutual lov
of screens and saw the concept as an area holdin
unlimited design possibilities.

The first two years were spent experimenting wit
various materials — papier mâché, glass, metal and wooc
Many new skills were acquired during this time, most c

SCREENS

...len room screens become works of art.

...em self taught. A set of wood carving chisels was ...ught following a lucky skip find of a large mahogany ...ardroom tabletop. This led to the creation of their first ...rved screen — L'Ocean. Since discovering that medium ...nsity fibreboard carves beautifully, they have con-...ntrated on the carved and painted image.

Bev and Mark have exhibited in Europe, USA and the ...me of the screen — Japan. Much of the work is ...mmissioned — by interior designers, architects and ...seums, as well as by private clients. At present work is ...derway on four screens for a London hospital.

The beauty of their work is quite stunning. The screens ...re one of the highlights of Creative Eye 1992 where ...ey evoked much interest and admiration.

Return by Mark Houlding
The carved line is emphasised with paint. The high gloss adds a luminosity reminiscent of stained glass

Lost and Found by Mark Houlding

Many of Mark's screens resemble wood and lino blocks, reflecting his interest in printing techniques. This screen was inspired by a visit to Japan. The contrasts found there are portrayed in the juxtaposition of roughly carved and smooth and shiny surfaces

The Bar by Bev Houlding

The human form is a favoured subject found in many of Bev's screens. The top of the screen is heavily carved to make the figures appear more prominent. Gold leafing has also been applied

Creek Bathers by Mark Houlding

Much of the carving was done after the painting, then coloured to highlight the crisp sharp marks

L'Ocean
The first screen, made from a mahogany boardroom table top

Technique
The design is carved into the surface of medium density fibreboard, which is then richly painted and textured, building up an intriguing ceramic quality to the look of the work. The screen is finally sealed with many coats of polyurathane varnish.

VINEYARD SCULPTURE

Norman Gaches had the task of transforming the broken stump of a wind felled tree into sculpture, as Mari Nicholson discovered.

Travel writer Mari Nicholson lives on the Isle of Wight with her husband Nick, whose hobby is sculpture. Watching him work has helped her acquire a technical knowledge of the skills involved in both sculpture and carving.

She developed a passion for woodcarving when she started travelling in South East Asia 15 years ago, and today she seeks out native carvings wherever she goes, to add to her collection. If she can't buy them, she photographs them!

A post-graduate student of Sussex University, she writes feature articles for a number of magazines both English and European, as well as short stories.

Her travel writings are all to do with the culture of the people she writes about. She is not interested in what she terms the 'sun, sand and sangria' scene.

It is an ill-wind that bloweth no man good, goes the proverb and the literal truth of this is to be found today on the Isle of Wight, in a magnificent carving that rises from one of the trees badly damaged in the gales that swept the South of England in 1987.

In the grounds of Barton Manor Vineyard, home of impresario Robert Stigwood, a family of Greek gods has been created from the remains of a one hundred and sixty year old Monterey cypress (*Cupressus macrocarpa*). Dionysus, Ariadne, and Zeus, plus the symbol of the Dionysian cult, a goat, now hold court on one of the lawns.

Norman Gaches, more famous for his marine carvings (such as the figurehead on *HMS Warrior* moored in Portsmouth Harbour), is the man responsible for these larger than lifesize figures. The tree, reduced to sixteen feet and tidied up after the gale, is still in situ — the roots being undamaged — and he made the first cuts on 16th October 1992, just five years after the gales. I asked Norman about the genesis of the idea.

Vineyard gods

'Well, the owner, Robert Stigwood, appreciating the commanding position of the sixteen foot stump, wanted something "Greek, but not too classical" in keeping with Barton Manor vineyards, and the idea of the gods seemed to rise naturally from the conversation between Mr Stigwood, vineyard manager Patrick Bywalski and myself' he said. 'It's difficult to say who thought of it first. The name of Bacchus was thrown up

and we took it from there. Dionysus as the discoverer of the wine was an obvious choice given the vineyard's increasing popularity as a producer of fine wines. The shape of the damaged tree lent itself to more than one figure so Ariadne as Dionysus's wife and Zeus, his father, were obvious choices. The goat, symbol of Bacchanalia, just followed on.'

Looking around Norman's workshop and flicking through his photographs of past work, the eclectic display of carving proves that he is not given to specialisation. Past and current work includes everything from marine figureheads, musical instruments, furniture and walking stick heads to this current piece.

At any one time he can be found working on four or five commissions, all at different stages of completion; ideally he would like to be involved on only one project at a time. 'That way you keep the enthusiasm going, especially with a large piece' he said. 'Besides, if the commissions are complicated, it isn't easy trying to keep the thought processes separate.'

The goat, symbol of the Bacchanalia

Dionysus, cup in hand, with Ariadne reclining behind him

Apart from the pleasure of carrying out such a commission, working on the tree was enjoyable for other reasons. 'Macrocarpa is technically a soft wood, fairly close grained and hard, but it's a pleasure to work with' said Norman. 'It's so beautifully scented.'

Unfortunately macrocarpa, like yew, tends to form bark inclusions as it grows. Digging out some early photographs, he pointed out the inclusions in this particular tree, some of them 12in deep. 'The design had to take account of this and it meant that I

The completed
sculpture of the
Greek gods
associated with
wine

had a few fill-ins as well. And obviously, there were one or two pieces of damaged wood to be removed,' he said.

The key element in Norman's work is his art. He is very positive that with carving, you must be able to draw it before you can carve it as 'the same image processes from the eye to the brain to the hand giving a similarity of style in both art forms.'

The plasticine model for Zeus

Method of work

In the case of this particular work he drew a basic plan of the tree's sectional shape, which gave him the pattern to which the design had to conform. He followed this with various drawings of the figures, working out the way he wanted to portray them. As is his usual custom, he then made individual plasticine models of all the figures, accurate to 1/10th scale, in order to familiarise himself with them in the chosen attitude.

'When working on large figures these models are essential for establishing proportions by measurement' he said. 'A design can be perfect from one viewpoint, but unattractive from another. Only by doing a mock-up can you be sure you've got a rounded design, one that is acceptable from all angles. And of course, it enables the client to see what the finished product will be like.'

Before starting the actual work, he takes measurements to make sure the proportions work out and then makes chalk lines on the block of wood.

You must be able to draw it before you can carve it.

'What' I asked 'is the most interesting part of your work, the conceptual, the research, the planning or the carving?'

'Definitely the conceptual' he answered without hesitation. 'That's when all the enthusiasm and ideas come tumbling together. It's got its own special kind of excitement. I have to see with my mind's eye the completed sculpture before I even touch the wood. Modifications are hard to make once the work is underway, so a predetermined plan is an essential. For instance, in the case of this commission I wanted to

convey the effect of a tree slowly becoming a person, the vine growing out of the tree, grapes in one hand, goblet of wine in the other. I wanted people to perceive instantly, almost intuitively, the connection between grapes and goblet.'

Dionysus, cup in one hand, grapes in the other

Detail of the grapes

gouging techniques to split off the wood and I do most of the roughing out with a 1½in No. 5 gouge. I've used this particular one every day for practically fifteen years' he continued, 'and it's probably sixty years old. The high chrome-like shine comes from use not a buffing wheel.' (The name Herring Bros. was still legible.)

Many of Norman's carving tools belonged to the famous sculptor William King and some of their handles still bear the marks of the fire which destroyed King's workshop during the blitz. 'There are fine carving tools made today' said Norman, 'but there's nothing to touch old English carving tools.'

I have to see with my mind's eye the completed sculpture before I even touch the wood.

I was intrigued by the rubber mallet which he was using and which he told me he's been using now for over 20 years. This particular mallet is extremely hard in appearance and feels like a composite of rubber and plastic. 'It's invaluable' he said. 'It was given to me by a German carver at Kiel and I've never seen another one like it. The rubber head helps to absorb the shock in the shoulder. A wooden mallet tends to mushroom and it destroys the handles of your other tools.'

I couldn't see a sander around so I asked how he smoothed the figures. 'With the tools with which I carved the figure' he said with a smile. 'Sometimes with a spoke shave. I prefer a more natural tooled surface texture, which I then finish off with linseed oil or beeswax.'

Method of carving

I spent some days watching him work at Barton Manor and became aware of the physical effort expended in carving such a large piece. In the Dionysus tree the problem is exaggerated by the angles at which he has to work, often having to cut upwards instead of downwards, placing an unaccustomed strain on his shoulder joints. 'After a few hours of this you know you've been working' he said. 'Being ambidextrous is one of the greatest assets a carver can have' he continued as he told me the story of a fellow carver whose apprenticeship was spent in a carving factory in Poland. 'Every thirty minutes a whistle was blown and no matter what stage the carving had reached they had to change hands immediately. Now he learned to be ambidextrous!'

Blocks, wedged into cracks that developed, carved to shape

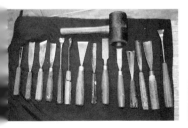

Norman Gaches tool kit, including a mallet with a hard rubber head

I was surprised to find that (apart from the most basic shaping), he used neither chainsaw, angle grinder nor router, preferring as he does to remove large areas of waste by controlled splitting. 'Those tools may speed up the work' he said 'but to me, the physical challenge to a carver is more in doing the whole thing with hand tools. I use

Norman Gaches had to use scaffolding to make this monumental carving

The smiling face of Zeus

Art, carving, spirit

Years ago men such as Norman Gaches were considered woodcarver tradesmen and I thought again of the old argument of artisan v artist. But looking at the gods that rose above us there was no doubt in my mind that here was a wood sculptor, an artist in his field.

A long time ago when the world was covered by vast tracts of forests, our ancestors believed that the trees were inhabited by gods and spirits. Today in parts of South America and in certain areas of northern Europe and Ireland trees are considered the home of spirits, demons and fairies.

And now, on the lawn at Barton Manor on the Isle of Wight, the gods once more take possession of a tree, thanks to wood sculptor Norman Gaches. ∎

Left **Occasionally Ricardo works to his clients' own design, with this Eygptian style mirror, carved from pine and jelutong (*Dyera costulata*), 8ft 6in, 2.6m high**

Above **Replica of a Greek marble sculpture, carved in Brazilian mahogany (*Swietenia macrophylla*), made from photographs supplied by the client. The original piece is in the British Museum**

Opposite top **A matching pair of armchairs made from yellow pine (*Pinus strobus*). Original design and execution attributed to Jacob Desmalter**

Right **Console table, possibly designed by Dominique Vivant Denon, carved in Brazilian mahogany and stands 33in, 840mm tall**

EN
UNITIES

Ricardo Rodriguez carves replicas of gilded antique furniture.

I first became self-employed as a woodcarver some thirteen years ago, more by chance than by design, after being made redundant from a firm of furniture manufacturers. From the beginning, most of my work has been related to furniture or fire surrounds, working for a fairly wide range of clients, including furniture manufacturers, antique dealers and specialist interior designers.

Top training

My initial training took place in my home town of Toledo in Spain, where I attended night classes at the local school of Arts and Crafts before moving on to serve a short apprenticeship with a local firm of cabinetmakers and woodcarvers. But it was only after I came to Britain that I realised that I could make a living from woodcarving.

By sheer good fortune, I met Gino Masero, a well-known master carver, and was able to observe him at work. Although my technique was fairly rudimentary, he agreed to take me on as a student, and he patiently taught me most of what I now know about woodcarving.

It was only after I came to Britain that I realised that I could make a living from woodcarving

It was through Gino's contacts and friends that I gained my first commissions. At first it was only simple carvings such as paterae and urns for fire surrounds. Later I did a fair amount of work for the College of Arms, some of which now stands alongside Gino's own carvings in St George's chapel at Windsor Castle and in Westminster Abbey.

Learning from past masters

Over the years I have specialised in making replicas of antique furniture and mirror frames, for which there seems to be a fair demand. Apart from providing me with a regular source of income, I often have the opportunity to study the techniques of great craftsmen of the past, while working from the original carvings. In most cases the quality of their work is absolutely immaculate, and one cannot help but feel very humbled by their mastery of design and execution.

Sometimes I have to work from photographs and, whenever this is the case I always advise the client that complete accuracy is almost impossible, which they usually accept. Providing I get a good selection of close-ups and accurate measurements to work from, I make every attempt to get as close as possible to the original.

Although it is fair to say that this kind of work lacks imaginative input it nevertheless demands a fairly high level of technical skill, as well as a good eye for detail.

Copying for profit

While I find most of this work very interesting and enjoyable, I must confess that I hate having to carve more than one foot of any particular moulding, which can be tedious at best. However, I have never been in a position to turn down work yet, and it pays the rent! ●

Ricardo Rodriguez is a member of the Master Carvers' Association and teaches private students in small groups from his own workshop. You can contact him at:
Hill Green Farm, Woodford Road, Poynton, Cheshire, SK12 1ED. Tel: 01625 871400

Above **Two griffins are the major feature in this limewood and pitch pine (*Pinus palustris*) consol table**

Left **A second Eygptian style mirror also made to the client's design, it stands 8ft, 2.4m high**

Below **One of three French Empire chairs made to complete a set. Design is attributed to Jacob Desmalter**

Whenever I work from photographs,
I advise the client that complete accuracy
is almost impossible

Arthur Koch

American sculptor Arthur Koch has created another collection of stimulating and varied new work, which visitors to Florence can see at the Romanelli Gallery, Lungarno, Acciaioli 74r, where he has a permanent exhibition.

Born in 1927, in Newark, New Jersey, Koch studied art at Trenton Junior College, taking his degree at the University of New Mexico. Since 1965 he has been working in Italy, and has exhibited in Florence, Rome, New York, San Francisco and Los Angeles. He shares his life in the countryside near Florence with his Australian wife and numerous cats.

Although he enjoys working in marble, stone (pietra serena) and terracotta, Koch predominantly works in the wood that yields the

AN AMERICAN IN FLOF

Eva Boyd reports on new work by sculptor Arthur Koch

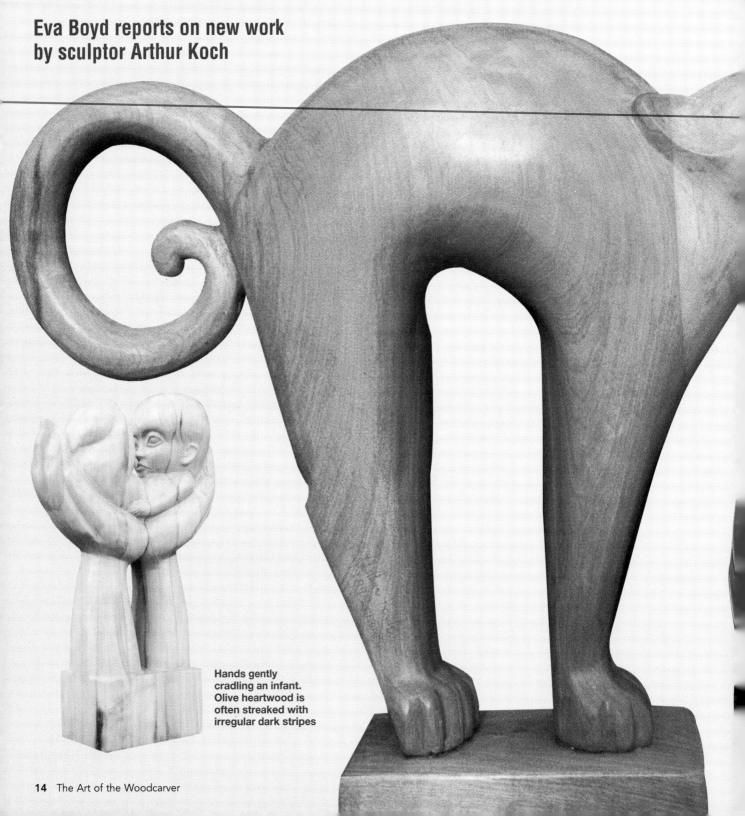

Hands gently cradling an infant. Olive heartwood is often streaked with irregular dark stripes

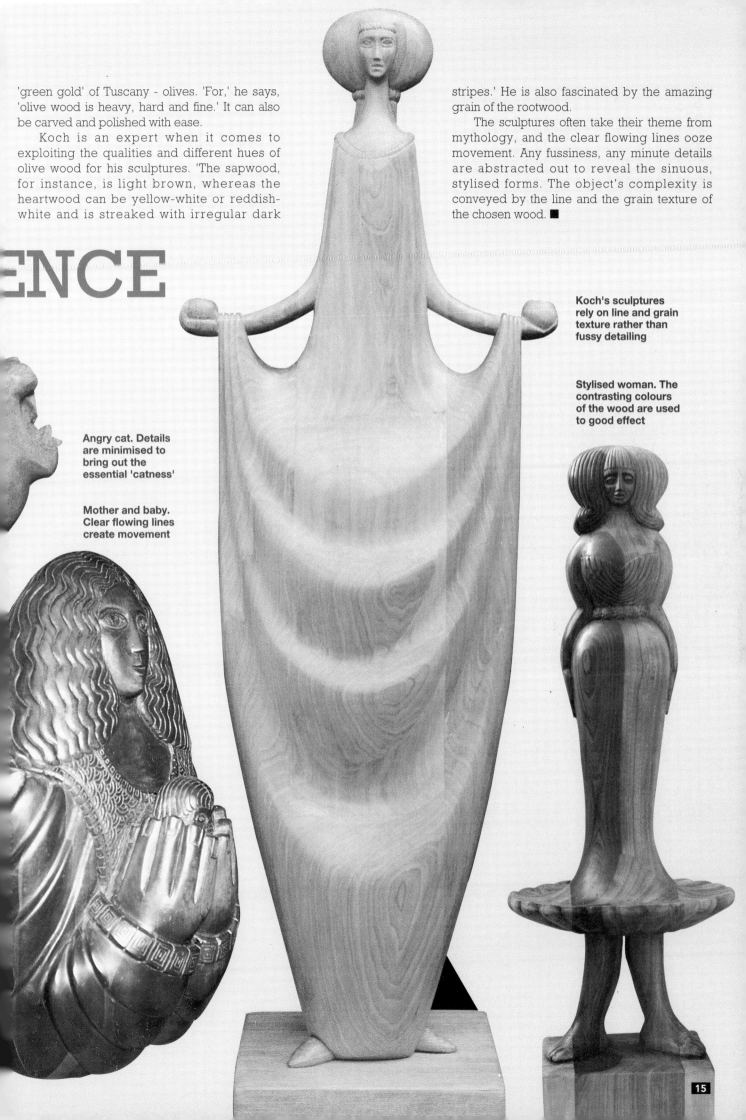

'green gold' of Tuscany - olives. 'For,' he says, 'olive wood is heavy, hard and fine.' It can also be carved and polished with ease.

Koch is an expert when it comes to exploiting the qualities and different hues of olive wood for his sculptures. 'The sapwood, for instance, is light brown, whereas the heartwood can be yellow-white or reddish-white and is streaked with irregular dark stripes.' He is also fascinated by the amazing grain of the rootwood.

The sculptures often take their theme from mythology, and the clear flowing lines ooze movement. Any fussiness, any minute details are abstracted out to reveal the sinuous, stylised forms. The object's complexity is conveyed by the line and the grain texture of the chosen wood. ∎

ENCE

Angry cat. Details are minimised to bring out the essential 'catness'

Mother and baby. Clear flowing lines create movement

Koch's sculptures rely on line and grain texture rather than fussy detailing

Stylised woman. The contrasting colours of the wood are used to good effect

The carver and a king

CONSUMMATE CRAFTSMANSHIP

TONY JAMES

Tad Mandziej is a world class carver who is perhaps better known abroad than in his home country.

In the kitchen of his cottage in a Somerset village, Tad Mandziej takes advantage of his wife Brenda's absence to gently cook a horse in the microwave oven. It comes out done to a turn. A small bird, however, given the same treatment, emerges charred and barely recognisable, and is consigned to the dustbin.

Tad Mandziej (pronounced Man-jez), whose Polish roots are now submerged beneath a slight west-country accent, is neither an experimental cook or a pyro-

Tad Mandziej deep in concentration at work

maniac, but one of the country's most gifted and successful woodcarvers. He is using the microwave to season the timber of his carvings.

It's a typical piece of technical expediency from a man who, despite a sound academic background, insists that he is a craftsman rather than an artist — a journeyman woodcarver — who treats commissions, varying from eight-foot high doors for a royal mausoleum to quarter-inch-high model railway figures, with equal enthusiasm.

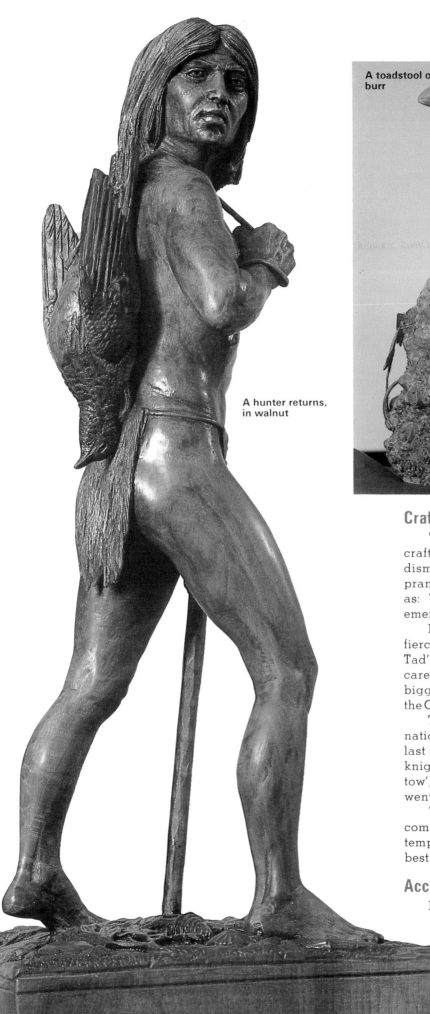

A hunter returns, in walnut

A toadstool on a burr

Craft and competition

'Nowadays I am really interested in craftsmanship rather than art,' he says, dismissing the 800 hours he spent carving a prancing horse out of a solid block of walnut as: 'Just chipping away until something emerges that looks right.'

But concealed under the modesty is a fierce spirit of competition, which influences Tad's approach to his craft more than he cares to admit. He was the champion of the biggest woodcarving show in the world — the Canadian National Exhibition in Toronto.

Tad's exhibits regularly win international and European competitions. His last major winner, which he decribes as: 'A knight on horseback with a slave-girl in tow', gave him a $10,000 first prize and went on sale for $15,000.

'I seem to have got caught in the trap of competition carving,' Tad admits. 'The temptation is to design things that have the best chance of winning.'

Accidental carver

In the low-beamed workshop at the end of his cottage, Tad sits impassively — as befits a man who also teaches philosophical Japanese martial arts — chopping his own brand of reality out of a brand of limewood.

He started carving by accident, while teaching textile design at Nottingham College of Art, and for the past ten years has worked as a professional woodcarver in Somerset. Now in his late 40s, Tad is obstinately rooted in the florid traditions of Victorian figurative art. His male figures are glossy and muscular and his women firmbreasted and defiant.

'People who pay big money for woodcarvings want things to be technically absolutely right. If you carve a horse you must spend weeks looking at horses and working out the anatomy.' And yet, reality is sometimes not enough — Tad recently turned down a lucrative commission to carve a nude from life, because the woman was too busty for his taste.

'I knew that whatever I did it would look wrong to my eye so in the end I had to refuse the job. I want to enjoy the things I carve.'

Art and competition

He's aware that he goes to Canadian and American shows with an inbuilt disadvantage: 'I'm too European for the north American market. If I carved cowboys and Indians or Canadian wildlife I'd sell them like hot cakes, but you'd need to be fantastically accurate.

'Out there, reality is more important than artistic merit. For instance I could

The carver describes this piece as a knight on horseback with a slave-girl in tow, in walnut

Combining mystery and craftsmanship

Photographs by Rob Cousins

carve a Red Indian which would be perfectly acceptable in Britain, but would be laughed out of the show in America. All they'd be interested in would be that a Cherokee has the third feather on the right sticking up not lying down!

'In the same way the criticism of my last winning carving had nothing to do with artistic merit. It was that the horse's back was too short. I knew they would say that, but there was nothing I could do about it. I had to change the design while I was actually carving because I struck a patch of rot . . .

'I don't like gimmicks, and that counts against me in competitions. Huge or microscopic carvings are popular at the moment. For instance, at the last Toronto show I judged, there was a toothpick with a ball and cage carved in it. Next to it was a 12ft tree-trunk in the shape of five eagles and a tiger. I like to carve pieces that will go into a suitcase!'

He will, however make exceptions, such as the four sets of exquisitely-carved teak doors, for the mausoleum of the English wife of King Hussein of Jordan, and the rose-festooned fountains, which stand in a palace in Oman.

'Most of my commissions come from people who have heard about me. If the jobs are interesting I'll take them, even though there may be problems.' For instance, carving tiny figures for a First World War tableau in the Imperial War Museum, taxed his eyesight so heavily that he finished the job working through two magnifying glasses tied to his head.

'If the jobs are interesting I'll take them, even though there may be problems.'

It was while carving a mask, which subsequently won a British competition, that Tad discovered that judicious use of the family microwave could season wood as effectively as the traditional natural process.

'I even merited four lines in *The Sun* newspaper, but presumably only because it gave them the excuse to use the headline "Oven Chippie".'

Country craftsman

The route to Somerset, and the apparently-idyllic life of a country craftsman, has in fact been long and traumatic for Tad. Born shortly after his mother escaped from a Siberian labour camp in 1940, he travelled with her on a gruelling eight-year trek to England, via the Middle East and Africa.

'It was in Africa that all our possessions were eaten by termites. We were put in a mud hut for the night, and in the morning all my mother had left in the world was the metal clasp from her handbag.'

In Britain, Tad learned English, studied art, and trained as a teacher. Today he regards the south-west of England as his spiritual, as well as his geographical home.

'I love the countryside and the wildlife, and particularly the plants. One thing I never tire of is carving a mushroom brought home from the fields on a summer's morning.' ∎

FIREBIRDS

Bob Swain carefully mixes his pallet of oil paints, then uses a small brush to add feather detail to the head of a black duck carving. He works quickly, and in a few minutes burnt umber feather edges run in a sweeping curve from the eyeline and down the neck of the bird. Suddenly Swain drops the brush, strikes a wooden kitchen match, and the head of the black duck erupts in flames.

Swain holds the carving over the concrete floor of his workshop, keeping it away from other flammables, and he watches closely as the orange flames encircle the head, then gradually subside and go out. He then picks up a paint-stained bristly brush and gives the head an enthusiastic buffing. After a minute or so of this, the remaining paint has a nice patina, and the bare wood shows through along the edges of the bill. The carving could be a century old.

Carving, painting, and setting birds ablaze is all in a day's work for Swain, a fifty year-old American who lives on a tributary of the Chesapeake Bay in Virginia. Seven years ago Swain gave up a garden supply business to concentrate on sculpting wooden birds. It was a move he has not regretted. After twenty years in a very competitive retail business, Swain relishes spending his workdays in his workshop overlooking Hunting Creek, a short boat ride from the Chesapeake.

Fire is a vital ingredient in Bob Swain's bird sculptures. Curtis Badger reports

Antique effect

'I have always liked old hunting decoys, and I began carving as an extension of collecting decoys,' he says. 'I try to capture in my carvings the elements I like about old decoys: the graceful form, the aged paint, the patina, the scars and nicks that tell you these carvings really had a function. They weren't made just to be put on a shelf and admired.'

After burning, buffing, and various other abuses, Swain's duck decoys definitely have a functional look. When he finishes the black duck decoy, it looks as though it could have come from a century-old hunting rig. But Swain isn't trying to dupe purchasers into thinking his carvings are antiques (he signs and dates each carving), he simply likes the well-worn appearance of old decoys.

Left **Great Blue Heron**
Above **Black Skimmers**

From top to bottom
● Bob Swain paints the black duck
● Setting the black duck ablaze
● Finished black duck

'I like the colour of old paint, but obviously I can't wait around for fifty years to get the patina I want, so I try to find ways to speed up the ageing process,' he says. 'I do things to a bird carving that would send fine woodworkers into shock.'

Natural inspiration

Swain's process begins with a chunk of white cedar (*Chamaecyparis thyoides*) and an idea for a particular design. Although Swain has carved numerous bird species, most of his subjects are the waterfowl and shorebirds that are daily visitors to the waters and marshes of Hunting Creek. Recent carvings include a cormorant with a fish in its beak, a hovering tern, and a lifesize great blue heron.

Swain begins by sketching the outline of the bird on the block of cedar, then cutting it out on the handsaw. The carving is done the old fashioned way, with a hatchet, a rasp, and couple of knives. When the carving is completed, Swain is ready to paint, but first he begins the aging ritual. Dirty paint thinner is applied to the wood, and it is set on fire, then buffed with a stiff brush. After several such applications, the cedar has lost its fresh-cut gloss and looks as though it has been floated in a swamp for the past hundred years. When Swain later removes or thins the paint, the "old" wood will show through, adding to the illusion of age.

Baptism of fire

The painting process involves fire and pigment; the paint is applied, diluted with thinner, and then is set on fire. When the fire is out, the area is cleaned with a bristle brush, and the process is repeated until Swain arrives at the desired colour and patina. Finally, the carving is scrubbed with soap and water, and then finished with a light coat of paste wax.

Obviously, Swain's burning technique has its dangers and drawbacks. If he burns too much, a decoy will more closely resemble a roasted marshmallow than a bird. And the very process of applying a flammable liquid to wood and setting it ablaze is extremely hazardous. But Swain is careful to burn only a small area of a carving at a time, and he does the burning well away from flammable objects.

'I studied with Mark McNair, who is a real master of aging wood carvings,' says Swain. 'Mark uses fire now and then, but it's secondary for him. For me, it's a primary technique. I use Ronan brand japan colours, which are very rich and thick. Burning and buffing seems to make them even richer, and the heat causes the wood to soak up the pigment. There also is an element of surprise because you never know exactly what you're going to get. You might get the look you want with one burn, or you might have to burn the same area three or four times.'

When Swain finishes a carving it not only looks old, but it also has a tactile quality. You want to pick it up and handle it, to turn it this way and that and study all the angles. 'That too, is one of the things I like about old decoys,' he says. 'Handling them is part of the fun of collecting them, and that's what I want my carvings to be like. If I'm at a show and someone comes by and picks up one of my birds, I consider that a compliment. I think any object that has good form pleases the hand as well as the eye.'

Swain spent more than twenty years attending to the needs of local farmers and gardeners at Economy Feed and Seed, Inc., a business begun in the 1930s by his grandfather. His clientele today range from coast to coast, and most of his business is done through wildlife art shows and through retail stores such as Lord and Taylor in New York City.

Bob Swain with a few feathered friends. Swain has been in a wheelchair since breaking his back in a car accident at age 20

'In a way, I'm still in the retail business in that I have to please my customers if I'm gong to make a living,' says Swain. 'But I'm not selling just a product, I'm selling something that has a lot of me in it. I make the best bird I can, and if someone wants to buy it, to make it a part of their home or office, I think that's very rewarding. If someone likes your work well enough to buy it, that's the sincerest form of flattery, isn't it?' ●

Top left **Dowitcher**
Top right **Courting terns**
Above **Shorebirds**

FRANK TRIGGS

The tradition of decoration on buildings is at last being used in contemporary style.

Frank Triggs runs a small workshop practice called Woodscape. Trained in painting and sculpture, he later gained a Master of Philosophy degree for his work in designing and building play environments for children and adults with severe learning difficulties. A self taught carver, he began by repairing antique furniture and, in the 15 years since, has rarely said 'we can't do that' to anyone who came through the workshop door.

His commissioned work has included furniture, architectural and figure carving. He has continued to make personal sculptural work since his art school days.

His main ambitions now lie in the development of contemporary architectural woodcarving, and he is actively seeking commissions in the area.

Nearly all of my working life is taken up by carving in one way or another. I want to communicate some of the exciting creative possibilities of using timber in contemporary decorative and expressive ways. The mass of people, when thinking of carving, think of a hobby for the retired, medieval misericords, souvenirs, Grinling Gibbons, the Victorian pub style, and Adam fireplaces — anything but the living form of the late 20th Century.

I do not wish to discount the work of the past, neither do I believe that it is necessary to go back to primitive crude work and re-invent carving. We have a whole range of wonderful traditional techniques from the simple to the sophisticated at our disposal. These are extended by new ways of doing things made possible by modern tools, materials and adhesives.

The important thing for me is creating something that relates to life today, whether it's a piece of furniture, architectural detail or a free standing sculpture. The *Light Pool* table I made was commissioned by West Midlands Arts, for the reception area of their Birmingham offices, following an open competition. I am fascinated by water, its movement, its moods, and wanted a focused image of a pool I had seen. Small dew ponds were once common in the fields before piped water was widely available in the country-side and the passion for drainage had taken effect. The one I had seen was perfectly round and clear and had a halo of leaves. I combined the idea of it with a light pattern I had seen in some slack water on a beach.

Using 12mm, $\frac{1}{2}$in intarsia for the centre of the table gave me room to produce the pattern of ripple in relief, to mirror the pattern of light delineated by the lime. The outer leaf pattern in holly, elm, robinia and walnut is 6mm, $\frac{1}{4}$in thick. When it came to final glue up, we dropped the lot on the floor; it took three of us an hour and a half to put it back together. The table edge is solid

cherry, the base is a torsion box of cherry veneered ply with an MDF core and solid cherry base and edging. The rippled centre section seems to detract little from its usefulness, at 1.3 metres, 51in diameter mostly people place their coffee cups and papers around its flat perimeter.

'My major interest is the development of carving in contemporary architecture.'

My love for moving water and the sea shows up again in the detail of a cabinet's doors; the ridged pattern in the walnut is based on a sandy shoreline after the tide has receded. The ridges were band sawn out and then individually power sanded with a foam drum held in the chuck of my lathe, before being cut in half and re-assembled on the ash doors. The holly 'shell' handles were hand carved then rolled over the surface of a hotplate to scorch the dark points round their rims.

Competition

Competitions can sometimes provide an impetus for experimental work. The promise of cash prizes, and the possibilities of having your work on show at an exhibition

ARCHITECTU

Below
**The *Light Pool*
table, to go in the
reception area of
West Midlands
Arts**

Below centre
**The intarsia centre
section is carved
in low relief to
represent water
ripples**

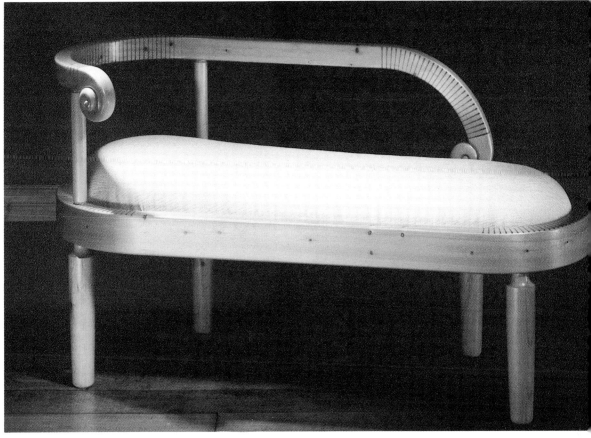

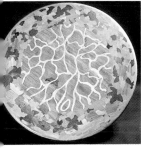

Detail of cabinet
doors, ash doors
with walnut
decoration and
holly handles

like Interior Design International, without having to pay for space, works wonders for enthusiasm. Such a competition was Imagine, organised by the Swedish Timber Council and the Chartered Society of Designers, with classes for furniture and architecture. The very open brief required innovation in the use of pine.

All timbers have their strengths and limitations: ordinary imported Swedish pine, the joiners' deal or redwood, is usually one carvers avoid. All your tools have to be super sharp and still the fibres will compress or tear rather than cut. It does, however, have lightness, warmth and translucency. Being a timber used extensively in building, it is one that someone interested in architectural work must come to terms with.

The small *Cornfield* chaise longue, which we christened the 'chaise short', was a form the workshop is fairly familiar with. We often have them in to carve or repair and I had thought many times of making a small version, with simple lines and restrained carving more to my taste. Kerf cutting gave

The *Cornfield*
short chaise
longue, kerf bent
and carved in pine

me a method of getting the curves without steaming and was a decorative element in its own right. The spiral shell terminal on the arm was a pig to carve, but is a joy to the hand when you are comfortably seated.

There was, unusually, enough time to make a prototype version, which ended up being painted to cover up all the experiments and changes of mind. This was subjected to ruthless criticism (and I thought they were my friends!) and several changes were made. I had expected the fabric for the seat to be difficult to find, but my local decorators' merchants came up with a beautiful shimmering textured material that exactly matched the lines of the timber.

In the architectural section I had no good examples of pine carving on buildings to show, so I decided that a model with supporting drawings would make the best submission. With such an open brief you have to take things step by step. An entrance is often used to define the function of a

RAL REVIVAL

building using decoration, but what sort of building? From a list of all the things I could think of about Scandinavia came the idea for a Marine Life Institute, with doors that were a cross between a breaching whale and a viking longship.

At one-fifth scale it is possible to carve the details quite finely in pine, lay the shingles properly and build the opening half-hull doors, even to laminate the structural beams. However, hot melt glue played a big part in holding the whole thing together, as proper joints were impractical.

Once the main door shape was defined, the roof line followed, then the wake in shingles and the planted bubbles, seaweed, fish and barnacles were added, and finally the shrimp hinges, which were carved in holly. A pine shrimp just would not cope with the hinge hardware inserted in its tail. Both the model and the sofa won prizes in the competition. The model was shown at Earl's Court at IDI in spring '93 and the sofa went to Copenhagen for the Scandinavian Furniture Fair in October '93.

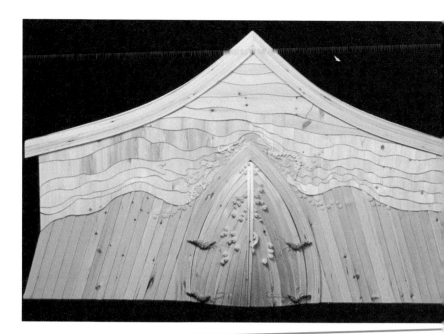

Decoration for a laminated pine beam, one side has oak and padauk sculpture inlay

Applied pine decoration on the other side of the beam

Laminated beams

Research for the architectural section of the competition led me up some very fruitful alleys. Glue laminated beams are used widely now in place of plain sawn beams from a single tree. I contacted several manufacturers of these beams to see if they knew of any examples which had been carved or decorated. No-one had, but Tysons Joinery in Liverpool, constructors of beams for the Thames barrage, offered me some sections to decorate for their showrooms.

An opportunity like this is very important for me. My major interest is the development of carving in contemporary architecture. As there are few examples existing, it is not surprising that few architects or potential clients are aware of the possibilities that exist, therefore little work is commissioned. The problem is how to break the circle: the opportunity to show samples in a prestigious firm's showrooms is one way, another is to enter drawings or models in competitions.

My sample beam has on one side a repeating leaf pattern carved in oak, let into the beam surface a little. Round ended padauk dowels make up the flowers. The other side of the beam has various turned and carved pine forms, planted on the face of the beam, grouped together to produce a varying texture.

The *Inner Space Woman* door goes back ten years. I had just finished a large, carved, split landing staircase and gallery, leaving a pile of nice offcuts of utile. Often clients baulk at the cost of hand work on larger projects and this was a trial piece, using cut and power sanded pieces to explore a cheaper decorative alternative. A simple but effective sculpted jig-saw was glued directly on to a veneered hollow core door.

Top
Model for a competition, a doorway for a Marine Life Institute, made in pine with shrimp hinges in holly

Above
Inner Space Woman, a trial piece using cut and power sanded pieces

Right
A swimming dog and an empty can provided the inspiration for *Last Unspoilt Wilderness*

Craftsmanship show

When Betty Norbury was compiling her British Craftsmanship in Wood Exhibition, she invited me to make a large piece for the exhibition. After some consideration of the available sites I decided upon the wall of the stairs leading up from a small room adjoining the main exhibition area.

I had been struck by the sight of a swimming dog and had made several rough sketches of that image. Then, on a long walk, having seen no trace of humans for some miles, I came upon an empty drink can. I put these two images together, having the can caught in an eddy of floating leaves in the dog's wake and called it, somewhat ironically, *Last Unspoilt Wilderness*.

The big sweep of the eddies was chalked out full size on the floor of the workshop, the shapes flowing down the stairs which were also defined on the drawing. I then chose boards whose grain pattern followed the shapes as much as possible, sometimes modifying the form to fit the boards. For such a big (8m x 4m, 26ft x 12ft) flat piece, fitting it together posed some problems. These were compounded by the fact that no fixings could be made in the walls of the exhibition area, so the whole structure had to hang from two brackets off the very substantial picture rail.

All difficulties were overcome however, and there it hung. I can only think that it fitted its place too well. It was with some chargin that I read one review of the show where the writer said how sad it was that there were no large scale or modern carved works. Thirty-two square metres and he hadn't seen it! It still seeks a home: several large banks, airports and financial institutions have turned it down, and not many places have a wall large enough to take it.

Last Unspoilt Wilderness, a sculpture made for the British Craftsmanship in Wood exhibition

The commission for Morrison's Supermarkets to commemorate the Sentinel Wagon Works in Shrewsbury is a recent work. There was a competition amongst Shropshire based artists for two works, my design being one of the successful ones. A mural form like this must have a strong composition for initial impact, and then plenty of detail to stand up to close scrutiny. There is everything in this one: painted MDF, dyed and natural veneer, dyed carved timber, straight high relief walnut figure carving, sculpted thick entarsia, assembled trucks turned and carved using natural timber colour, and resin inlay. We even sneaked in the carvers' names on the truck sides. It was tremendous fun, virtually problem-free and all done with totally marvellous wood.

Wood

Wood is such a sensual, warm, friendly material. It gives an enormous range of possibilities to someone who wants to use it expressively. I hope to see it used more extensively to decorate buildings as we move away from the soulless buildings of the recent past. Architectural scale means that for the carver there is more to consider. The interplay of light and shade in the forms of the work and the lighting of the piece gain in importance. Composition and the rhythm of repeated forms, the visual effect of large areas of flat or textured timber, its stability, even its durability. All these considerations, and more, combine to make carving a totally absorbing art. All of us are doing our bit to add to our craft. I hope showing some of my work has opened up a few more possibilities for you. ∎

This relief carving for Morrison's Supermarket in Shrewsbury commemorates the Sentinel Wagon Works

A variety of materials was used to create visual impact and interesting detail

REBUILDING THE BATAVIA

Re-constructing an East Indiaman involves considerable woodcarving as Francesca Runting found

n October 1985 the keel was laid for the construction of a replica 17th century merchantman, the Batavia. The project is to build the ship as authentically as possible and to provide training for young people in shipbuilding, rigging, sailmaking and woodcarving.

The wreck

The event which led to years of planning and research, was the discovery of the wreck of the Batavia in the 1960s, off the west coast of Australia. The Batavia, carrying thirty-two guns, was a heavily armed, three masted merchantman with an overall length of 185ft 8in, 56.6m. She was built in Amsterdam in 1628 by the Dutch East India company (the VOC) to carry goods between Indonesia and The Netherlands. The VOC was a very large and extremely profitable company contributing to the 17th Century wealth of The Netherlands with an impressive fleet of ships.

On her maiden voyage from The Netherlands to the former Dutch East Indies in 1629 she went off course and ran on to the reefs of West Australia.

Most of the crew and passengers managed to reach a few little islands, but in the mutinous aftermath over half the three hundred and sixteen men, women and children who had been on board died.

Shipwright's dream

Willem Vos, a builder of traditional Dutch style boats, had a dream to build a Dutch East Indiaman before the Batavia was found. Building such a vessel would be an opportunity to learn more about the ships

The Batavia spring 1994

An oak Batavian warrior nearing completion

and would preserve many traditional skills in danger of being lost. Years of research and planning began.

Slowly Willem built up an archive. The wreck of the Vasa also proved to be a valuable source of information. Although Vasa was a Swedish man-o-war she was built in the same year as Batavia by a Dutch shipwright, and is now preserved in Stockholm.

The remains of the original Batavia, preserved in the Western Maritime museum in Fremantle Australia, gave technical information with regards to the hull shape but there was not much to work with.

Fortunately Willem was able to determine the outside measurements of the ship from the original charter from 1626, ordering the building of the Batavia for the VOC.

Reconstruction

A building site on the shore of Ijsselmeer was donated by the town of Lelystad and investors provided starting capital. Willem Vos was able to lay the 121ft 5in, 37m long keel of a Dutch East Indiaman, on October the 4th 1985.

In 1987 Cees van Soestbergen, a woodcarver with many years experience in the restoration of buildings, took on the task of researching, designing and creating the 200-250 carvings for the Batavia.

Since none of the original Batavia's carvings had survived, much research work was needed to build up a picture of how the Batavia could have been decorated. Files of photographs were compiled of the ornaments adorning 17th century buildings and contemporary

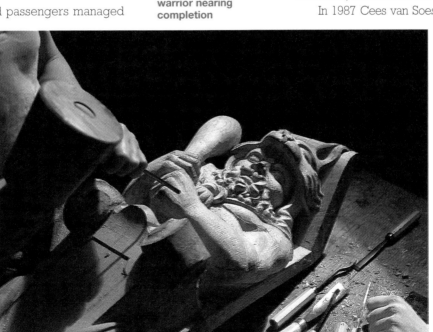

One of the oak
Batavian warriors
on the stern

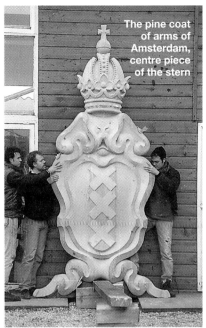

Oak scale models of two of the figures from the stern made prior to carving them full-size

The pine coat of arms of Amsterdam, centre piece of the stern

Carver's apprentice

In the Batavia yard to be accepted for training in woodcarving you have to make a test piece. You are given a photograph of a 17th Century carving, a piece of oak cut roughly to size and tools. Cees van Soestbergen doesn't expect a perfect reproduction, what he wants to see is a true attempt to reproduce the style and expression of the original.

First a line drawing is made, taking into account the size of the wood and the proportions of the original in the photograph. It is useful to have photos of front and side elevations, so certain depths can more easily be estimated. The line drawing is then traced on the wood using carbon paper, and the basic profile can be set in.

Keeping a good centre line on the wood is important, especially in the early stages – it serves as a reference line to check the position of features against your drawing. When everything seems to be in the right place the drawing

prints line the walls of the woodcarvers workshop.

Research goes on and is shared by Cees' pupils, who, as part of their training, are responsible for designing and creating particular carvings.

I joined the Batavia project in December 1990 and with the temperature outside at -8°C I was relieved to be offered a place in the sail loft. I spent a year and a half learning traditional sailmaking and acclimatising myself to the world of ships.

During that time I became increasingly fascinated by what was going on in the woodcarving department and, having come to the conclusion that I didn't want to become a sailmaker I decided to have a go at carving.

Pupils are surrounded by prints, plaster copies and models of late Northern Renaissance work

The four oak statues as they appear on the stern of the Batavia

becomes less important and the photograph and your intuition take over.

At this stage one of two things tends to happen, either you rapidly come to the conclusion that you never want to see a woodcarving again or – like those of us who made it into the workshop – you become increasingly fascinated with your newly acquired skills. There is no time limit put on the test piece but those who do finish their carving (about 80%) tend to take two to four months to do so.

Once accepted for training a second test piece is made under Cees' supervision. The basic elements involved in this particular style of woodcarving are practised without the stress of working for the ship.

The workshop

The workshop is furnished very traditionally and pupils are surrounded by prints, plaster copies and models of late Northern Renaissance work. In this way you are influenced by the feel and style of the 17th century, to carry this through into your work. The workshop has its own library with books explaining the style and its characteristics – examples to draw ideas and inspiration from.

The tools used are to a large extent traditional, with all carving work done by hand. In the early stages of a particularly large piece such as the lion figurehead, pneumatic tools may be used. The machines are from the Atlas Copco range but chisels and gouges are specially forged for the workshop. The use of machines is kept to a minimum as the noise disturbs the other carvers.

The carving tools in the workshop, some one hundred and fifty in all, are of Dutch and German origin. This collection contains many of the more unusual forms and sizes and is intended to complement the basic sets of about thirty tools that pupils are encouraged to build up themselves. I recently introduced gouges made by Henry Taylor and Ashley Iles into the workshop, both makes proving very popular.

Sharpening is done firstly on an electric grindstone and then the burr is removed with an Arkansas stone or Belgian sandstone in water. We finish the edges on leather dressed with Vaseline and emery powder. Another popular method of sharpening tools is the cloth dolly. The philosophy in the workshop is that although a well honed edge is quickly achieved, contact between carver and tool is lost.

The carvings

Because no drawings or paintings of the Batavia exist an impression of the decoration had to be built up from contemporary examples. It is not possible to say that the final result (as far as the carvings are concerned) is a reproduction of the Batavia of 1628 but it is a good impression of

how she could have been decorated, based on all the information available to us.

The embellishment of the stern is on the theme 'Batavia'. In 17th century Holland a parallel was sought between the revolt of the Celtic Batavian tribe against the Romans in 69AD and the revolt of the Dutch republic against Spain during the Eighty Years War (1568-1648).

The stern

In the middle of the stern, between the leaded windows of the Captain's quarters, are statues of Julius Civilis (also known as Claudius Civilis) the legendary leader of the Batavians, and his co-patriot Brinio. To show the comparison they are accompanied by the leader of the Dutch revolt, William of Orange and his son Maurits. Directly beneath these are half figures of Batavian warriors and a cartouche surrounding the VOC insignia with the letter 'A' representing Amsterdam: one of the six VOC authorities and where the Batavia was built.

One feature until recently missing from most of the figures around the stern were the pupils of their eyes. These were set in on completion of the stern following a plan that ensures that all directions are 'under surveillance'. This is a feature that Cees van Soestbergen discovered on the Vasa – it was probably for superstitious reasons.

The carvings high on the stern have been carved in larch and pine to keep them as light as possible so as not to affect the stability of the ship too much. The stern is crowned with two heraldic dolphins flanking the medieval coat of arms of Amsterdam framed with a carved rope.

The figurehead

The lion figurehead is made from limewood for crispness of detail, but also for its relatively light weight since it is positioned right at the end of the beakhead. The open frieze on the beak is carved in oak.

Most of the carvings had no real function other than to impress friend or foe. They may have given peace of mind to the crew, who may have believed that the mythical beings and grotesque faces would protect them from

Top **The lion figurehead is the only limewood carving on the ship**

Below **The lion figurehead being carved, in the background the Batavia under construction. Photo courtesy of the Batavia yard**

One of the oak knights that decorate the pulley sheaves

The magnificent stern of the Batavia

misfortune. However, there are some functional carvings. Knights' heads protrude through the decks with sheaves of pulleys underneath them for the rigging.

With the exception of some of the stern carvings and the figurehead, all the carvings are made in oak. Where possible one single massive piece will be used. The rough block is made to fit in position on the ship before carving, sometimes leading to problems with holding the work. Special supports are made for pieces with hollow or round bases.

The oak used is from Denmark and, like

Knights' heads protrude through the decks with sheaves of pulleys underneath them for the rigging

the wood for the rest of the ship it is unseasoned. There are problems with splitting as the wood dries and larger cracks are filled with wedges of oak that match the grain glued in place. Smaller splits tend to close up when the finished carving is coated in boiled linseed oil.

All the carvings will eventually be gilded, or painted using oil-based colours, but not until they're all completed. More research must be done into colouring. For the time being linseed oil and a base coat of paint provides protection and carvings in position are regularly given an extra coat.

The future

With the launch date of the 700 tonnes Batavia set for March 1995 and with about thirty carvings still to be made for the exterior alone we have an awful lot to do. After launching, the Batavia will be moored close to the yard and work will continue for several years.

Apart from receiving acclaim and support for its training programme the Batavia yard has about 350,000 visitors a year, making it financially viable. Now the project will continue into the next century.

Plans have been finalised for the building of a second ship in the yard. This will be the 'Zeven Provincien' (Seven Provinces), she was built in 1665 and was the flagship of Michiel De Ruyter during several of the Dutch wars. Being a man-o-war she will prove even more of a challenge to shipwrights and woodcarvers alike and will safeguard the future of this unique project for many years to come.

British Batavia

There is some concern in Britain that traditional skills are decreasing to the point where they may be lost and expertise would have to be imported for major restoration projects. With this in mind a project on the same lines as the Batavia is being contemplated in Britain. If realised it would involve the training of apprentice woodcarvers and the making of hundreds of Renaissance woodcarvings. Anyone interested in finding out more about this concept can contact: The great ship 'St. George' study group, The Old School Bungalow, Gisleham, Lowestoft, Suffolk, NR33 8DU. ∎

Francesca Runting is 23 years old and was born in Oxford but raised in Gisleham near Lowestoft. She left school to become an actress, playing Pandora in 'The secret diary of Adrian Mole' that toured Britain. She played in several other UK productions but left for The Netherlands with her Dutch fiancé. Both started to work at the Batavia yard in 1990.
Initially Francesca worked as apprentice sailmaker for one and a half years, but for the last two years she has been apprenticed as a woodcarver under Cees van Soestbergen. She has made several pieces for the Batavia including the crowning piece for the stern. Francesca has also managed to extend her acting career and has appeared in a Dutch-Canadian television series.

LIFE'

Sculptor Michael Fairfax describes his work as project artist for the seaside town of Weston-super-Mare

Light and Shadow is the name I gave to a series of six sculptures sited around the resort of Weston-super-Mare in the South-West of England near Bristol. They were executed between 1993 and 1994 when I was employed as project artist for the town. This meant I worked three days a week for the local district council under their Tourist Development Action Programme. South West Arts part-funded the project, and encouraged the council to institute a public art scheme.

Seeing the light

The seafront at Weston boasts 2½ miles of beach and thus a lot of sky, and the sun sweeps around the beach from dawn to dusk. I walked around the area many times, noting the movement of the sun, possible sites for the sculptures, and buildings and other landmarks that I could use as imagery for the carvings. I wanted all the carvings to have a pierced form to let the sun through in one way or another.

During this exploration I discovered that three of the niches I had decided to use create an amplification of the voice. By standing at a given spot and talking out to sea, your voice is projected back in both ears. This was an added bonus, and I made off to my studio in the old town quarry doubly happy. I set to work on a series of drawings, bringing in the distinctive characteristics of each site.

Site one

This alludes to a lighthouse on the distant island of Flat Holm in the Bristol Channel. It has a carved image of another island, Steep Holm, and the light pours through two strong vertical lines which bear witness to the vertical lines of the posts on the nearby causeway. All I had to do was to bring these together into a cohesive image.

Site two

In this sculpture the top part represents the distant land mass of Brean Down, with more verticals of the causeway. There are six, and the light really shimmers through them as the sun sets on the sea.

The carved wave pattern comes from the stone balconies on the Ocean Hotel behind.

Again these are pierced and people can look through the holes, either at one another, as they seem to take great delight in doing, or at the sea.

Main picture
Site one: Steep Holm
Left
Site two: Brean Down

Chainsawing the timber

Site three

More than the others, this piece has a contrast between the surface texture of the chainsawn wood and the vertical line which the light blitzes through. The top is taken from the shape of a nearby shelter, but generally I have left more of the shape of the original tree.

Site four

In the far distance, standing on the hillside, is the church at Uphill. There are two carvings of scratch dials on the wall of the church – ancient marks which were used to tell the times for Mass and Vespers with the help of a gnomon, the stationary arm which projects the shadow.

This imagery has been used for the fourth sculpture. Light comes through a small hole in the centre of the horizontal line.

Site five

More abstract, and slightly oriental in feeling, this sculpture overlooks some large rocks which are often used for sunbathing. They have deep fissures in the surface, and I have copied a section of these lines, chainsawing and carving them onto the wood. Here again the horizontal line lets the light through.

Site six

The capstones topping the seawalls in Weston are wonderful, beautifully eroded by water, salt, wind and rain. This last piece is a celebration of them, and of the joy of sculpture. It is also the largest in the series, standing 8ft, 2.5m high. On the dark side are three spiral carvings leading to the holes of light.

Model beginnings

I ordered seven pieces of cut oak, 10ft, 3m high, minimum 6in, 150mm thick and 18in, 460mm wide, from Treework Services in Backwell. The timber, large and green, was delivered to my studio.

For each piece I first made a maquette to hone down the finer details of composition and mark making, which proved particularly useful. I

Wooden maquettes used to work out details of composition and carving

I was spellbound and as soon as I got back home I set about making a boat-like sculpture which I burnt over a fire. The piece is called 'The river ran dry'. That was the start of my playing with fire. Over the ensuing years I have mastered the techniques so that I'm not left with a pile of ashes. Now I have four different burning nozzles, from large to a small jet for getting into small holes. I also use a paintbrush and water to stop some areas burning more than I want.

The real thing

After I had finished the maquettes, I set about the real pieces. For the first month I had the help of a student, Paul Needham, doing a placement as part of his course on 'Art in a social context'. I used a petrol chainsaw with a 14in and 18in bar. I find it much easier working on this larger scale as I don't chase the wood around the studio – because of the weight, it stays put! The six pieces took about three months to complete.

As with the maquettes I charred the surface and used a wire brush to remove the char, followed by rubbing down with coarse wire wool which creates a brown colour. I then treated the wood with teak oil to reinstate the black effect I wanted.

I am looking forward to seeing how the sea air and water affect the wood – the splitting, cracking and discoloration.

An unveiling ceremony took place in the autumn of 1994. We promenaded from sculpture to sculpture, with a traditional jazz band evoking scenes of New Orleans. The sun shone and the sculptures looked brilliant. Oh the joys of being a public artist. ■

used a 12in bar on an electric chainsaw and my normal woodcarving gouges. All verticals were done with the tip of the chainsaw.

Burnt offerings

Once carved, the maquettes were charred. I have been charring wood since 1986 after I saw the Amazon exhibition at the Museum of Mankind in London, a favourite haunt of mine. They showed a film of the Amazonians at work: they cut down a tree, adzed it out and then built a fire and burnt the canoe very slowly over it. After that they quickly put the seats in: the wood contracted as it cooled so the seats were held firmly in position.

Michael Fairfax, left, and student Paul Needham on charring duty

Michael Fairfax did a foundation course at Portsmouth College of Art and completed his BA in Fine Art at Newport, Gwent in 1980. He is a committed environmentalist and works with stone and wood, usually on a large scale, creating pieces that complement and enhance the landscape. Commissions throughout Britain have come from, among others, regional arts associations, the Woodland Trust, Sustrans and Forest Enterprise. Michael has also worked in Italy and the USA

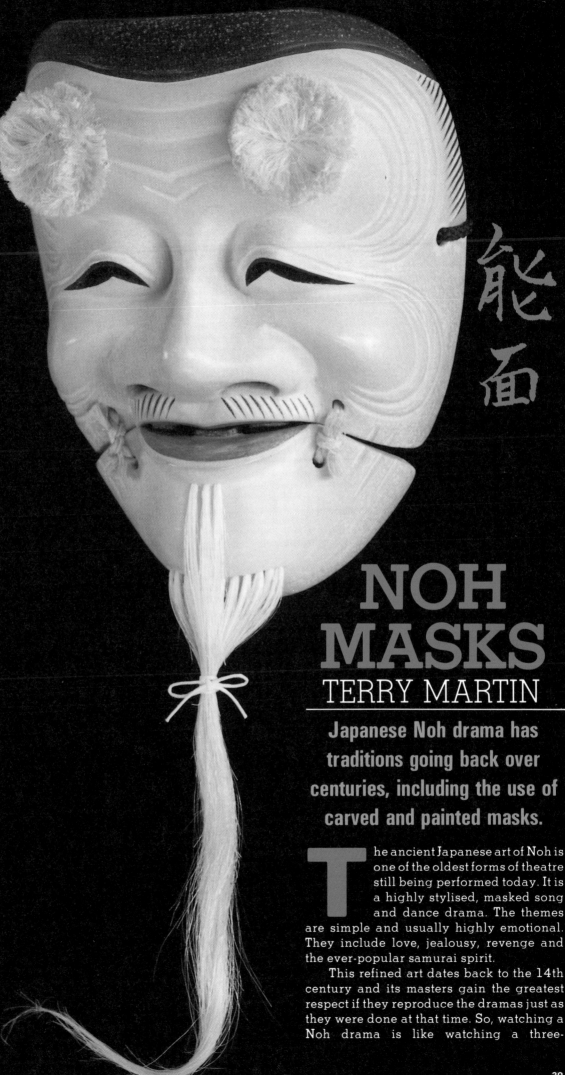

Terry Martin was born in Melbourne in 1947. A graduate of Armidale College, Adelaide, and the University of New England, New South Wales, he has had a satisfying and adventurous life travelling the world in various capacities, including Stage Manager of the Royal Opera House, Covent Garden, Ski Patrol in Austria, geological exploration in the Pacific Islands and Migrant Education in Australia.

A growing appreciation of fine craft work was heightened by several years spent in Japan and when Terry returned to Australia he decided to pursue his interest in woodcraft.

Terry believes that woodturning allows us of limited timber resources for maximum effect. Much of the wood he uses is recycled, such as fence posts or railway sleepers. Influenced by Japanese ceramics and other crafts, he believes that the natural faults of the timber should be allowed to remain to enhance the work he does on the wood.

Old man mask

能面

NOH MASKS
TERRY MARTIN

Japanese Noh drama has traditions going back over centuries, including the use of carved and painted masks.

The ancient Japanese art of Noh is one of the oldest forms of theatre still being performed today. It is a highly stylised, masked song and dance drama. The themes are simple and usually highly emotional. They include love, jealousy, revenge and the ever-popular samurai spirit.

This refined art dates back to the 14th century and its masters gain the greatest respect if they reproduce the dramas just as they were done at that time. So, watching a Noh drama is like watching a three-

The basic outline for a small mask is cut from quarter sawn stock

The sides are roughly bevelled leaving a high strip for the nose

The brow, mouth and chin areas taken down

Side view showing how the shaping progresses

The nose roughly shaped, a high area is left for the lips as the mask is rounded

Shaping continues, the forehead is more gently curved th the chin

Takatsu-san at work

小面制作図

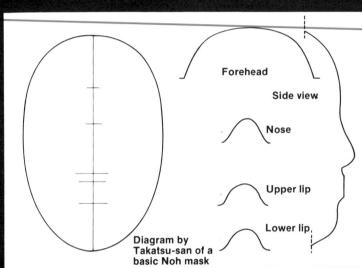

Forehead

Side view

Nose

Upper lip

Lower lip

Diagram by Takatsu-san of a basic Noh mask

dimensional time capsule. The costumes, voices, language and movements are all as they would have been at that time. To put it into perspective, imagine if we could watch Shakespeare *exactly* as it was done in his time — except Noh is over two hundred years older than Shakespeare.

One of the strongest impressions of Noh comes from the masks worn by the main actors. Although all of the actors are male, they take the roles of female characters as well as demons, ghosts, and so on. All of this is done by change of costume, voice and mask.

As a result of many years experience in the theatre, along with the fact that I speak Japanese, several years ago I was asked to be Australian tour manager for the Kanze Noh group of actors. Members of this family are all descended from the original Kanze who founded Noh theatre in 1333. The master at the time of the Australian tour was the 36th Kanze in line from his famous ancestor. To use the Shakespeare analogy again, imagine meeting the direct

descendant of Shakespeare who was still performing the plays as his ancestor had done!

After we had been touring for some weeks I was invited to enter the Kagami-no-ma, or mirror-room, where the main actor dresses before the performance. This was a great privilege and I was introduced to the ritual of placing the mask on the face. Surrounded by younger actors, the main character is dressed in layer upon layer of the fine silk costume, some of them very old.

Then the actor contemplates his own appearance in the mirror for some time, meditating and breathing slowly. When he is ready he indicates that he wants the mask. With an atmosphere of reverence, even awe, the mask is taken from its box and unwrapped. The actor bows his head in greeting to the mask and puts it on.

Until that moment he is himself, but once it is on he considers himself completely transformed into the character of the mask. The actor believes that he puts his whole self into the mask.

Nose, eyes, lips
and chin refined —
the chin stands
quite high above
the jaw line

The cheek curves
down from the eye
to the lips then to
the jaw line

Features finished,
the whole mask is
sanded ready for
painting

The nose and
mouth are well
defined to be
easily seen on
stage

The back of the
mask, the maker's
mark inside the
forehead

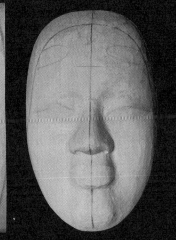

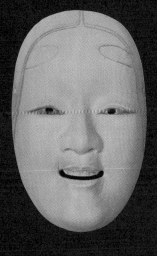

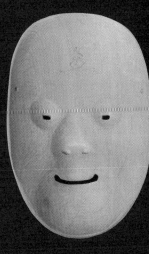

Maskmaker

What kind of masks hold this kind of power and respect? Who makes them and how are they made? As we would expect, many of the maskmakers are descended from other maskmakers. Last year I was introduced to one man who makes masks for the Kanze family.

Takatsu Koichi is unusual in that he was not born into a maskmaker's family and his children are not continuing in the work. Born in 1941, he started carving Noh masks in 1964. To show how slow the rise to accepted status is, his first solo exhibition was not until 1986.

The small mask completed

In 1989 one of his old-man masks was placed in the Hiratsuka Hachiman shrine, a place of great significance in the tradition of the art. In 1990 he was particularly favoured by the Kanze family with the use of one of his masks for a special performance which was broadcast by national Japanese television. In 1992 one of his masks was part of an exhibition of superior Japanese craft at Barcelona. Also in 1992 he was given high recognition by his local government for his contribution to the craft.

Takatsu-san makes his masks from Hinoki (Japanese cypress) which are generally around 300 years old. Special trees in Japan are earmarked for temple construction, carving and other fine work and are nurtured for centuries to this end. They don't take the short-term view of such matters in Japan! He particularly favours the Kiso and Bishu varieties of cypress as they are very durable and water-resistant owing to the natural oils in the wood.

The billet of quarter-sawn wood is split into 300mm, 12in long pieces and then sawn into the oval face shape. The sides are bevelled and the brow and mouth sections are cut away, then the face is rounded with the gouge. After refinement of the eyes and nostrils, the outline of the hair and eyebrow 'make up' is drawn on. The eyes and mouth are then pierced through for vision and voice.

The very small mouth hole muffles the actor's voice. but this contributes to the other-wordly feeling of many of the plays. It is interesting to compare the size of this mouth hole to the quite large holes in Greek theatre masks. It was sometimes claimed that the mask was an amplification device in Greek theatre. This could never be said of the Noh mask where the actor has to strive to project his voice to the audience.

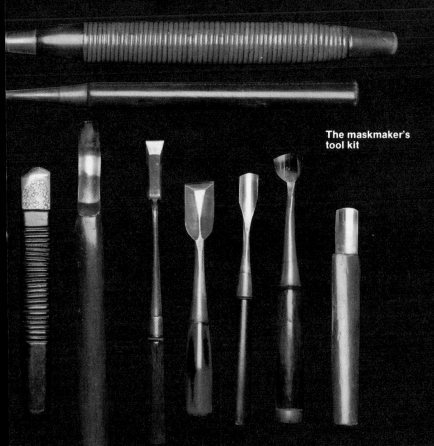

The maskmaker's tool kit

oyster shell powder is laid on the mask and the inside is finished with lacquer. Then the colours are mixed with the same oyster shell powder and many layers are painted on to give depth to the finish.

Many masks are carved with a neutral expression and the emotions or other nuances are added by the actor through the angle of head, use of light, voice, and carriage. Exceptions are the old-man masks which have the lower jaw carved separately and hinged with strings. The eyebrows and beard are made of stiff hair imbedded in the wood. Both have expressions of hearty laughter — open mouths and narrowed eyes. Demon masks are, of course, given a frightening expression. ∎

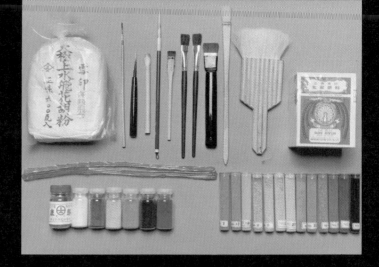

A child mask

The untidy hair and strange teeth and eyes show that this is the mask of a demon

A more obviously demonic mask

TREE OF CAYLAR

Suzy Placet describes the extraordinary elm carved by Michel Chevray

The beautiful Herault department of southern France boasts a regional curiosity in its Larzac area which never ceases to intrigue all those fascinated by woodcarving.

Many French villages in the last century still had an elm tree planted in the main square. Although this tradition has disappeared, like most of the trees in the 1980s after Dutch elm disease ravaged the area, one 100-year-old elm escaped the axe, thanks to the town council's initiative and one man's imagination.

Life restored

It was in 1987 that an artist from Brittany was appointed to fulfil what must be every woodsculptor's dream – carving life into a dead tree. The talented Michel Chevray worked from April to September in 1988 and over the same period in 1989. After 2000 hours, he was rewarded by the enthusiasm shown by the visitors who come in droves to marvel at this monumental testament to patience and talent.

During the two seasons in which he worked on the tree, Michel Chevray attracted many admirers. People would come to watch the

Above *The Tree of Caylar*, protected from the elements in the middle of the village square

Below **Detail of the shepherd's head, with a lamb over his shoulders**

Overleaf **Another shepherd with his dog, and a woman, possibly a muse**

master at work, staying for hours at a time. Often these encounters with travellers or local inhabitants were the source of further inspiration.

Drawn from Nature

The trunk depicts two shepherds, one carrying a lamb on his shoulders and the other accompanied by his dog. Above him is a voluptuous woman, possibly a muse. Among the toads, mushrooms,

Villagers were so delighted that they have built a shelter to protect it

horses, foxes, owls and wild boar can be seen a naked Christ-like figure wearing sunglasses, and a strange death's head.

There is also vegetation in the form of flowers and wheat and a giant thistle – a traditional symbol of Larzac. A huge ram supports the upper branches which are laden with figures, and the whole is topped with a lavish cockerel. The work is so intricate that the more you look at it, the more you see.

There remains one branch, however, which has been left untouched. A homage to the tree's

An eagle, squirrel
and lizard decorate
the upper branches

An owl perched
in a hollow

natural origins and a delicate gesture on the part of the artist, it gives the visitor not only a strange desire to get out his carving tools, but also a sense of the size of the gargantuan task undertaken by Michel Chevray.

Pride of place

The village of Caylar lies on the N9 road between Millau and Lodève, and is well worth the visit if ever you find yourself in the region. It's easy to find because the villagers were so delighted with their 'chef d'oeuvre' that they have built a grandstand-type shelter around it to protect it from the elements.

It also has a low balustrade to prevent the amateur enthusiast whipping out his penknife, an act which would be criminal but understandable in the circumstances, such is the urge to get cracking oneself. So, before felling that old dead tree at the bottom of the garden, why not think about the possibilities of bringing it back to life again? ■

The work is so intricate that the more you look at it, the more you see

SKULLPTURE

Roger Schroeder talks to Greg Krockta about the skulls he carves from burls

Some people call Greg Krockta's skulls macabre. Others accuse him of skulduggery – a forgery of sorts. But to Krockta his sculpture is an art form which uses the gems of the forest. "People mistake these for real skulls," he says, "and maybe there's some unintentional skulduggery in that. But what I'm after is not really skulls but sculptures that use burls."

Krockta, who lives on Long Island, New York, USA is an artist and also a professional sign carver. He says burls offer an ideal combination of material and subject matter. They have the kinds of defects and flaws that an old skull would have. Even the colours and grain patterns are characteristic of an old skull which has been buried in the earth.

What exactly is a burl? Krockta says tree experts describe a burl as a tumour or cancerous growth. It seems to be a random occurrence which is not caused by human intervention. Little research is available on burls and any information he has found has been no more than a paragraph or a chapter in a book.

Krockta agrees with the experts that a burl is a growth in which the cells grow out of control, much as they do with a human or animal tumour. But, he says, "There is never anything wrong with the burl wood. I find it living and thriving. Some theories say a burl will kill a tree, but that may be because it's stealing too much life from the tree."

Among the redwoods of California, burls are not only common but, when at the base of the tree, give off new growth. They ensure the continuance of the tree if the main trunk perishes.

Wood search

Living in the northeastern part of the United States, Krockta feels he is limited by the kinds of burls he can use for his sculpting. The three most common burls, he says, are found on oaks (*Quercus spp*), maples (*Acer spp*) and cherry (*Prunus spp*).

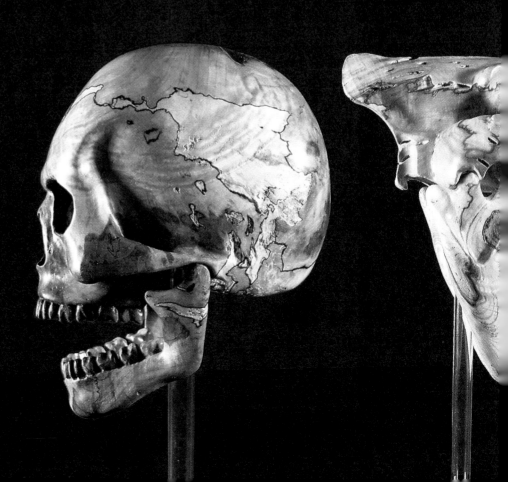

> Burr hunting is part of the process... It's a thrill finding something so scarce

Far left **A human skull, made from a spalted maple burl.**
Left **A lion's skull from a silver maple burl.**
Above **A springbok, carved from a maple burl with curly maple horns darkened with an ebony stain.**

As far as hardness is concerned, oak and cherry seem to be consistently more uniform and denser than the maple burl. But maple in his area tends to have soft spots because of spalting. This is caused by water getting into the wood. He rarely sees spalted oak or cherry burls.

The burl he now favours is from the maple tree. Admitting he is bored with the cherry burl, he feels his best work is done in maple. There are over six different varieties growing in the northeastern area of the United States.

Krockta travels great distances in search of a burl for two reasons. One reason is burls are not common occurrences. The other is he refuses to purchase a burl.

He elaborates, "You look and look and finally you see one on a country road and it's like finding gold or a gem in the forest. But to most other people it's something unsightly and useless.

"Burl hunting is part of the process," he says. "I've looked for them on private properties, in parks, on country roads. It's a thrill finding something so scarce. But it's also fun getting out the chainsaw and sometimes going 50 feet in the air with a ladder to remove a burl. It's definitely a masculine thing to do."

Inspiration

How did Krockta get started as a skull sculptor? He says it began with a small cherry burl he had under his workbench. A friend had come for a visit, picked it up, and asked if it was a skull. Krockta answered no. But he was immediately inspired to carve the burl into just that. Six years later he visited American wood sculptor Armand LaMontagne with the burl skull in his pocket.

Almost shyly he showed the piece to LaMontagne, who was impressed. He not only encouraged Krockta, but also gave him eight burls to take home and carve.

Krockta waits at least a year for a burl to season before he starts to shape it into a skull. After that he finds an appreciable weight reduction. He prevents premature cracking by leaving the bark on the burl.

Primary research

While his burls are drying, Krockta is doing research. This includes not only reading but also visits to museums and to a firm in New York City that sells and rents skulls. Called Maxilla and Mandibles, this enterprise caters to sculptors, filmmakers, students, artists or anyone interested in skulls. It claims to be the only business of its kind in the world.

Feeling he does not have to invent anatomy if he has the real skull in hand, Krockta often rents a skull. He then shoots several rolls of film, both colour and black and white. Next he takes measurements and examines the shape with his hands.

The first step in creating a sculpted skull is matching the burl with the subject. Krockta explains "the more you can fit the shape into the burl, the better off you'll be. That way you won't be wasting something so precious. And with skulls that's not too difficult, since most burls are roundish or oblong."

Next he draws up a pattern which he puts into an opaque projector. This enables him to reduce or enlarge the pattern slightly so it can fit the burl.

He says slightly bigger is better, adding that "small subjects don't show off the busy grains and colours of a burl." When he is finished, he is usually within 1in, 25mm of the outside diameter of the burl.

"I spend a lot of time trying to envision how the skull

will look in the burl, and a lot of time is also spent running between the burl pile and the opaque projector," he says. He justifies his size adjustments, saying that what he is creating is art, not something for an anatomy class requiring exact dimensions.

He draws as many views as he thinks is necessary. They may include one or both side views, a top view and even one for the bottom.

For a human skull, he wants only a front and a back view. For a buffalo skull he will draw only a top view. "That's the whole shape," he says. "From the front you see almost nothing." He draws only what he is going to carve.

Krockta says he does not get overly involved with details, with the exception of the teeth. A skull, he points out, is not that detailed to begin with. This makes burls an ideal medium because details would be broken off or visually lost given the irregularities of the material.

Shaping

He begins carving with a chainsaw. Describing it as a sculpting tool, he feels he can step back and see his progress better than he can with a bandsaw. But he may spend no more than an hour shaping with the chainsaw before he goes to smaller and even more powerful tools.

When Krockta made that first skull out of his cherry burl, a piece he now describes as primitive, he used an electric drill and a rotary rasp to shape the wood. Today he uses compressed air. "Air tools tame the wood," he notes, "even overpower it." Using a 5 hp compressor, he has no trouble shaping a burl's varied textures and differences in density.

He says flexible shaft grinders are neither fast nor safe for sculpting burls. A jammed tool in this kind of grinder will keep on rotating. But a handpiece for an air compressor stops almost instantly, once the hand-held lever is released. Electric grinders, with their rheostat boxes or hard-to-reach switches, are not so easy to stop. "Air power is always at your fingertips," he points out.

Even delicate areas such as teeth are better handled with the high speed of air-powered bits running at 35,000 rpm. Krockta says teeth would probably be broken off by a less powerful tool which is forced into the wood.

One of Krockta's primary tools which is adaptable to the air compressor is the rotary carbide rasp. Able to cut fast and cleanly, the head of this rasp is made up of needle-sharp points of tungsten-carbide.

They come in a variety of shapes, sizes and grits. They can be round, cylindrical, tapered and bullet-shaped. Their diameter can span less than a ¼in, 6mm and the grits include 80 and 120 grit. Whatever the size or shape, these rasps can do a great deal of wood removal while leaving a fairly smooth surface.

Sanding

When it comes to sanding, Krockta puts aside the air compressor and picks up a flexible shaft grinder, the very tool he shuns for wood removal. A sanding attachment powered by air will cause the sandpaper to tear apart or rip the grit off it because there is too much power.

Krockta says sanding is a big part of working burls. "It's boring, it consumes hours, it's messy. But the big pay off is when you get that nice smoothly polished burl." His favourite sanding attachment is a ¼in, 20mm diameter cushioned drum sander. He says sanding bands, with their hard rubber drums,

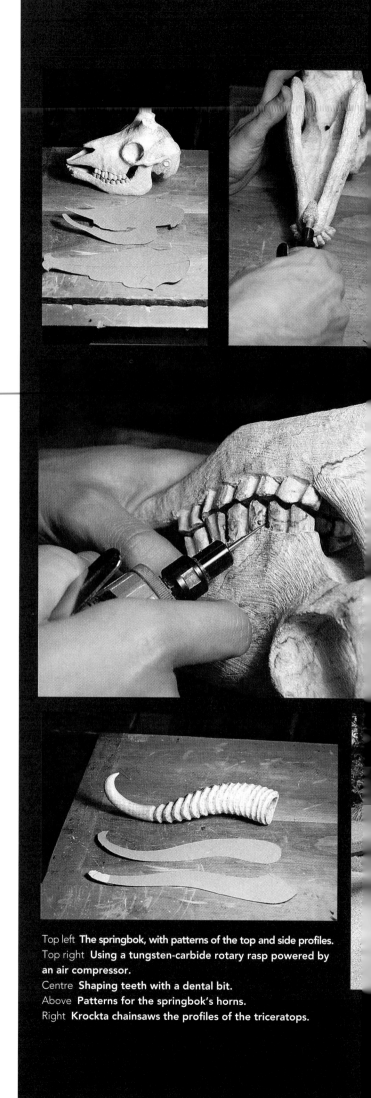

Top left **The springbok, with patterns of the top and side profiles.**
Top right **Using a tungsten-carbide rotary rasp powered by an air compressor.**
Centre **Shaping teeth with a dental bit.**
Above **Patterns for the springbok's horns.**
Right **Krockta chainsaws the profiles of the triceratops.**

are too rigid and tend to gouge the wood.

When sanding, he begins with 100 grit aluminium oxide cloth paper. This will take out the marks left from gouges and rotary rasps. From there he progresses to 150 grit and then to 220, which he feels is sufficient since he is not staining the wood. When making horns, he increases the grit size to 320.

Sometimes the cushioned drum sander is too large for the nooks and crannies of skulls. For those he makes his own sanding attachments, using tubing or steel rods wrapped with foam rubber shoe inserts and sandpaper. Another homemade sanding attachment is a solid rod with a slot through which he can attach a piece of sandpaper, which is then wrapped around the shaft.

Cushioning the sandpaper is crucial, he explains, because without it the grits come off the paper or cloth too quickly. Finishing a burl skull takes many hours of sanding, especially without some kind of power tool. "I can't imagine sanding burl without power," he says, "especially in three-dimensional sculpture."

Despite the diminutive size of some of his carbide rasps, these are not the smallest tools Krockta uses. He also employs dental bits supplied, of course, by his dentist. These are effective when giving definition to the teeth of a burl skull.

Experimentation

Most of his finishing work is done with brushing lacquer. He favours it because it dries quickly and can be rubbed smooth with steel wool. Presently, he is experimenting with the surface of the wood. This means not putting colour into the wood, but taking it out.

He explains, "Most woodworkers go natural or stain or paint. But I take colour out of the wood for a special effect. Using a bleach, I can make a dark wood lighter, or even make it look like another material such as stone. That's what you get when you bleach." Laundry bleach has little effect on wood, so he uses a two-part wood bleach.

He is also experimenting with sandblasting the surface of a burl skull. Sandblasting gives a pitted, slightly textured effect to the surface, making the burl even more skull-like.

The hours of research and hard work have paid off with impressive sculptures. The cherry burl skull was one of several human skulls he has done, including one of a prehistoric man.

One of the more interesting pieces is a modern day human skull in spalted black maple (*Acer nigrum*). Krockta says it looks great, "but it was a hard burl to work. The spalted part was considerably softer than the rest of the wood. I literally had to float over that area with the tools. But you'll never find another burl like that one."

Taste for teeth

Exploring the evolutionary ladder of man, Krockta did a chimpanzee's skull from a red maple (*Acer rubrum*) burl. "I was interested in where we came from, especially since we are 98% genetically identical to the chimpanzee." He adds, "I like the fact that they have pretty impressive teeth."

Krockta soon discovered there were other animals with impressive teeth. His lion skull, inspired by a book on animal skeletons and made from a silver maple (*Acer saccharinium*) burl, has a ferocity accentuated by the prominent canines. "It's a dramatic piece," he notes, "impressive because of the large and menacing teeth.

"Without teeth and horns, skulls can look boring," Krockta says. And so he moved on to other game animals. "I started off with human skulls, then prehistoric skulls, then animals with horns. It was a natural progression," he explains.

One of his first was the springbok, an African gazelle with horns which curve outward and inward. This, too, is a maple burl with the horns carved from curly maple. To darken the wood he used an ebony-coloured, alcohol-based stain.

Another African animal done by Krockta is the impala. Sculpted from sugar maple (*Acer saccarum*), its horns of curly maple are an impressive 22in, 560mm long. A reason for choosing this animal was that he was able to get an impala skull as a reference.

One of the largest skulls he has done is the American buffalo, or bison. This one measures 24 x 28in, 610 x 710mm and was sculpted from a red oak burl.

Explaining why he chose this subject, he said the buffalo was the most recognizable skull in American art, one which had been used by Native Americans in rituals for thousands of years. "And it's probably the most popular animal skull in the United States," he adds.

Krockta is now looking for new subjects to sculpt. One of them is the dinosaur. He likes the size of big dinosaurs, their unusual appearance, and their new popularity. Is he daunted by their size? His answer is no, but he adds, almost thankfully, "You can't get much bigger than that." ●

Roger Schroeder is a prolific writer and lecturer on woodworking, construction, sculpture and carving, as well as a cabinetmaker and amateur carver. He combines these activities with a full-time job as a high school English teacher, specialising in teaching creative writing and research.

Paul Warner's earliest interest in art was as a painter of landscape and abstracts based on Dorset life and scenery. He became interested in wood carving when working for a degree over 20 years ago. Feeling the need for a more physical release than was afforded by painting, he bought himself a set of tools, obtained some timber and began.

That was over 20 years ago. Since then he has taught Design, specialising in wood, both in schools and adult education centres. Last year he took early retirement in order to concentrate full time on his creative activities.

From the outset his inspiration has been drawn from the natural world, particularly the landscape and birds around him, but his approach has nearly always been to interpret through abstract forms rather than to copy slavishly and naturalistically from nature. He attempts to convey the spirit of something through its form as freely and creatively as possible, and would feel constrained by a more figurative approach.

SHADOWS ON THE HILLS

PAUL WARNER

Sculptural carving inspired by a remarkable group of hills and their history.

Many years ago I was travelling back from Scotland to my home in Dorset. I was tired, and my children were practising walking up and down my spine through the back of my driving seat. From the motorway close to Worcester, I saw what I then took for a range of mountains rising from the Severn Valley. Shadowed, they stood out irresistibly against the early evening sky. Beckoning.

I had to stop and park the caravan for the night. It was either that, permanent back injury, or infanticide. I headed for those 'mountains'.

The following day I walked the Malverns for the first time, and began a love affair that, with a sprinkling of fate thrown in, led to my becoming a resident some years later, the owner of a Victorian cottage and workshop high on the eastern slopes close to the Wyche.

As a committed landscape photographer and sculptor, it was clearly only a matter of time before I used the hills as the subject matter for an exhibition. Oddly enough it took several years to really get going. This was partly because I held a teaching position that increasingly drained me, and partly because I wasn't really sure how to approach the task. Simply representing an area visually isn't really my scene. I like to look for a place's essence, its spirit. Although the Malverns are clearly and self evidently beautiful, I have always felt conscious of something deeper within the region, and I wanted to explore that aspect more than any other.

With this in mind I have consciously tried to avoid the obvious and the simply picturesque. I decided to photograph in black and white, itself an abstraction, in order to provide a graphical backdrop for a group of sculptures made from wood. I find that one kind of creative activity often feeds another. When out capturing images with my camera I get ideas for sculptures. When carving, the opposite often happens.

Inspiration and interpretation

Within the group of wood carvings that form the sculptural content of a recent exhibition, I found that the work quite readily fell into three related groups:

a) the 'substance' of the hills, such as rocks, trees, pathways, plants, winds and waters;

b) a still continuing exploration of the hills' creatures, mainly the birds which either reside or visit;

c) the least tangible part, that of trying to evoke my sense of the hills' distant past through a series of 'druidic forms'.

I have met many people who have experienced a sense of unease in certain parts of the area, particularly towards the southern end, around Raggedstone and White Leaved Oak, where there is reputed to have been a Druidic temple. This is a quiet corner still claimed by many to be haunted. It's certainly quite lonely down there at times when the mists rise and the shadows lengthen. Who knows?

All of the Druidic forms are both literally and metaphorically ambiguous, and as such are really quite difficult to write about since they are intentionally mysterious and reflect fragments of the hill's history, very old and shrouded in mystery. The dualities, spirituality and carnality, the blade and the wing, are quite deliberate.

Very little is known of Druidism in the Malverns, except that it was almost certainly present. My approach is essentially

The Pool Bird.
440mm, teak on lime. The hills have many enclosed, secret waters; deep, dark pools formed in old quarries. At times, birds of all sorts, including some quite unlikely species, might be seen skimming the surface seeking food. Bird and water sometimes seem to meld together. This one is an abstract of them all, my pool dancer

Top left
Hawk above the spring. 485mm, mahogany on oak. Characteristically, the open hillside features several pure water springs, famed for containing nothing at all (unless the sheep get there first!). Hawks are often to be seen hovering above these. The water has travelled up from deep beneath the rock and meets the sentinel above; two freedoms signal briefly to one another. As usual I have gone for abstraction, trying to marry the two forms as a unity of sorts — a metaphor

Top right
Wind, Rock, Woods and Water, 553mm, mahogany and apple on ash. From Wynds Point and Hereford Beacon through to Raggedstone there is a magical mixture of scenery, including the now well publicised area recently chosen as an impromptu festival site by New Age travellers, Castlemorton Common. This is a kind of sculptural 'sketch'. I probably ought to mention that I don't normally design and make a carving, then put it on a base, but much prefer to create each piece as an integrated whole

Centre left
Druidic form One — **Harmonies.** 525mm, mahogany and sycamore

Centre right
Druidic form Two — **Fate.** 522mm, oak and lime on bog oak

Bottom left
Druidic form Three — **Secrets.** 610mm, oak and lime on ash

Bottom right
Druidic form Four — **Knowledge.** 520mm, lime on bog oak

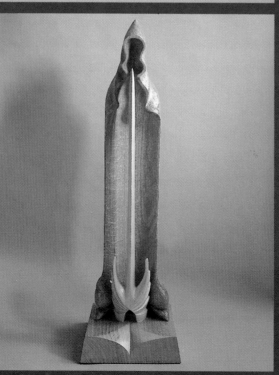

imaginative, based on intuition rather than fact. I have tried to carve into wood the feelings and emotions which I have experienced whilst wandering around and photographing in some of the more isolated parts of the hills. Sometimes my thoughts have soared exultantly, experiencing a tremendous sense of vitality and release, and at other times I have felt quite threatened and vulnerable. At all times I have felt that these two emotional extremes were, in fact, intertwined — somehow one and the same.

Panelpieces

On Panel three: **Dreaming in the grass,** the base of the mount carries a fragment of a 14th century poem called *The Vision Of Piers Plowman*. Its author, William Langland, is said to have fallen asleep by a spring beneath British Camp, the ancient Iron Age fortress that dominates the central section of the hills. His dream became his poem. In part I have tried to reflect his picture of the hills as being dualistic and paradoxical in character, soporifically beautiful but also containing ominous layers 'beneath the surface, "with deep ditches and dark and dreadful of sight".

There is also another, rather more prosaic, element involved. The hillsides suffer often from fires, especially in a very dry season, and I found myself photographing the regeneration of plant life, particularly the spear-like grasses so characteristic of the area. They are here in the carving, sometimes masquerading as the flames themselves and, paradoxically, rising above the hillforms.

As a technical aside, I have overcome some of the limitations of relief carving in this piece by making the 'grass' from two relatively thin sheets of lime which I then joined together, leaving a narrow gap between the two to create an illusion of greater depth. However, when doing this sort of thing it is of course important to remember that wood moves.

To pin two such pieces together without allowing for shrinkage would be to court disaster almost as soon as the work reaches a centrally heated environment. The easiest way to do this is to mount the spacers along the grain (assuming, of course, that the grain on both runs in the same direction). However, this could allow the material to bow, therefore mounting across the grain is structurally more satisfactory. This is fine providing that the spacers' screw holes are slotted to allow sufficient movement. Remember, even so called dry wood can shrink by a quite alarming amount, often because the worker doesn't allow for the amount of moisture that kiln dried timber can absorb during storage.

At present I have one further panel planned within this project. When showing visitors the work I had completed so far, I was delighted to be given a commission, a personal work for them, but one they want included in the exhibition. This pleased me greatly as, for some reason, I have always found relief carving peculiarly satisfying and absorbing. Perhaps it's because my early interest in art was as a painter. Also odd is the fact that relief panels seem to sell much more readily than a free standing sculpture. Perhaps it's an abiding tradition in this country that 'art' is something that you generally hang on the wall. If something is three dimensional it is meant only for public places like galleries, not homes. But then, by and large the British public seems always to have resisted the notion that original art of any sort can be safely domesticated — house trained even!

Choice of materials

With a couple of exceptions my choice of materials has favoured home grown woods. I like that kind of conscious symbolism. It pleases me to think that most of this timber came from not that far away. In the case of the bog oak, it might well have been forming whilst some of my druidic subject matter held sway amongst the hills' most ancient inhabitants. It's also worth adding that air dried native timber is much sweeter beneath the tool than anything that began life a thousand miles away, and ended it in a kiln!

'I have tried to carve into wood the feelings and emotions which I have experienced whilst wandering around and photographing in some of the more isolated parts of the hills.'

To date I have secured several exhibitions throughout the West Midlands, including a tour sponsored by the Hereford and Worcester Library Service, commencing in the spring. In addition there has been some interest from outside the area, and, hopefully, I will be obtaining more venues later during the year. In the meantime, there is framing and carving to be done. Back to the workshop!

Panel one:
Treeforms.
795mm overall,
apple on a painted
MDF mount. I do
like relief carvings.
This one was
actually inspired
by a series of
photographs that I
made, also for the
exhibition, of
woodlands at the
south end of the
hills. Ancient
survivors of the
old Malvern
Chase, I find these
woods
tremendously
evocative of a kind
of timeless
tranquility and
peace, just
occasionally
tinged with
mystery and
unease. I have
tried to convey
this as well as
evoking the
rhythmic qualities
of form and light
and shade found
between the trees

Left
Panel two:
Treefringe.
630mm overall,
ash on a painted
MDF mount.
Although similar
in inspiration to
panel one, this
carving has more
to do with the
edge of the wood,
where two worlds
rub together and
complement each
other, blending,
and yet somehow
always managing
to remain as
discrete entities

Panel three: **Dreaming in the grass**. 630 overall, sycamore and lime on a painted MDF mount

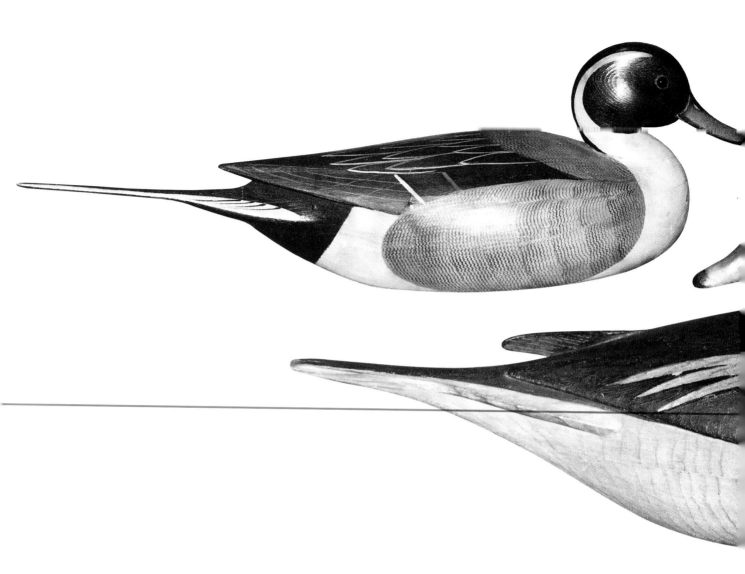

MODERN CLASSICS

Mark McNair has developed his own distinctive style of carving traditional decoys, as Judith Nicoll discovered

n my first year of carving in 1987 I was lucky enough to travel around the eastern shores of Maryland and Virginia, where there is a strong tradition of carving decoy ducks. With the eye of the uninitiated I found many of the old decoys oddly shaped and even ugly. At the opposite extreme was the breathtaking realism of the detailed birds, which could only be admired but never aspired to.

In between I found several carvers who follow decoy carving in its traditional and evocative form but who have evolved their own style and skills. They have hardworking, professional attitudes I can relate to and skills that are easy to understand.

Among the best of these is Mark McNair, whose carvings are superbly constructed with clean graceful lines. His craftsmanship has been highly influenced by past decoy carvers but he has never copied. He speaks with deep respect for the old methods of carving and painting, and having worked with him I know that every carving is given the time and care it needs for perfection.

Happy hunting

Decoys and hunting are a way of life in this part of the world and many of Mark's carvings are made to be shot over. He calls himself a Connecticut Yankee who came to the eastern shores about 16 years ago to carve. His house overlooks a creek on the Chesapeake Bay where he hunts. He believes that carving decoys makes hunting a more rewarding experience; and that hunting has enhanced his knowledge of the birds and given him a different feel for what he's doing. 'There's a tremendous satisfaction to take a piece of wood, fashion it into a duck, take a rig of these out into a marsh and have wild ducks pitch into it. It's really fantastic.'

However, Mark does not carve his decoys as just birds to throw on to the water. He works to create something pleasing to the eye; his painting exceeds the requirements of a working decoy. Nor when carving any bird does he limit himself to a certain quality and think of a price. Rather he approaches carving as an art form, because that's how he was introduced to it and, he says, 'that is my motivation to stay with it'.

He believes carving decoys makes hunting a more rewarding experience... and hunting enhances his knowledge of the birds

---

Mark is an artist as much as an artisan, and he sees putting life into a decoy as a sort of alchemy. Serviceable decoys can be made with a lot of practice and hard work, but not everyone can put life into them. Much of this ability is due to intuition and an intimate knowledge of the bird, combined with satisfaction at doing a job well. 'It should be built with integrity, like a boat, it should function.'

Materials and tools

Mark works mainly with Atlantic white cedar (*Chamaecyparis thyoides*), which is durable, locally available and has a pleasant aroma. For inserted bills and tails he might use white oak, or ash (*Fraxinus* spp). He finds there is nothing

Top left
Painted pintail by Mark McNair, completed in 1987. Note how the patterns of the painting complement the three-dimensional shape

Top centre
Grain is used to emphasise the shape and to resemble feathers

Top right
Widgeon, painted in mellow colours that give the impression of age

Far left
Hunting is a way of life! Mark McNair shooting crows from his workshop window

Top left
Taking a class, Mark McNair demonstrates hollowing out the top half of a pintail

Centre left
Student rounding out the body with a rasp

Bottom left
Getting to grips with a drawknife

Right
The hollowed bird in two halves

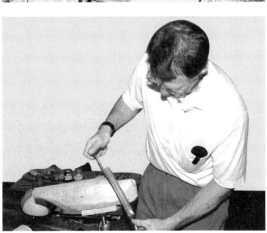

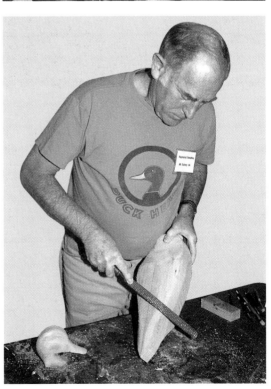

quicker than a hatchet to rough out the bird. He uses an old lath hatchet, sharpened with a bevel on one side, but also has a variety for different purposes. Pupils in his classes soon adapt to the hatchet, though I admit to struggling when borrowing Mark's bevel for left-handed use.

Cabinetmakers' or pattern-makers' rasps are used for shaping and finishing, leaving a rough rasped texture. His UK pupils use the

Nicholson 49 and 50 rasps. Also recommended is a good moderately-sized drawknife and a Stanley 151 spokeshave.

Mark has Ashley Iles chisels, his first choice being 16-20mm skews. Size obviously depends on the size of birds, but he believes in using the largest tools possible because they help create long contoured planes and stop you getting hung up on detail. He likes to use 'long continuous strokes rather than picking away with a knife'. His sharply cut name on the bottom of the carvings is done with an awesome 4½in, 115mm long knife – a favourite is from the Swedish company Frosts of Mora.

Work in progress

Long experience enables Mark to draw birds directly on to the cedar before bandsawing. The body is cut out of two pieces temporarily screwed together for carving. Once the body is roughed out, he separates and hollows them with a drill press or scoop chisel. Hollowing balances the bird, as well as making it lighter and preventing the wood from checking. He gets a kick out of seeing how thin he can make it.

Once hollowed and left with a ½in, 13mm rim, the head is attached from the inside with a brass screw, and the halves are glued, clamped and tacked.

Below
Insetting the tail

Below right
Pinning the two halves together after clamping

Shaping a bird is a question of mapping the high points and coming down from them, turning the bird constantly to make it pleasing to the eye from all angles. When carving the head he thinks of the bill as part of the skull and uses the grain to accentuate the form and to resemble feathers.

Complementary colours

The overall design of two-dimensional paint should enhance the three-dimensional shape, the graphic pattern of one accentuating the planes of the other. Mark seems to look for patterns and shapes in the colours, a good example is all the triangles in the shape and patterns on the pintails.

Most of Mark's pupils are new to paint, and find it the most difficult aspect to master. He encourages people to use their imagination, not

Painted and unpainted pintails completed in 1993

to copy, and he himself is constantly experimenting.

He works with oils, painting directly on to the surface without sealer so the paint soaks in. He mixes up a primer with the oils and blocks in main areas of colour, then draws on the patterns in pencil for the other colours.

Mark uses oil paints and varnishes creatively to produce textured surfaces and different tones, for example by dry-brushing Van Dyck brown over black, or dragging a metal comb through a top colour to reveal a base colour below. His birds appear to have a 50-year-old patina: he does not antique them, he paints them in mellow colours and then tones them down. One of his favourite colours is Terreverte, a swampy brown.

After my course with Mark I bought various cans in lovely subdued tones of Japan colours from the Mohawk and Ronan paint companies. These dry quickly to a flat lustre, are lead free, and can be thinned with mineral spirits. (A set of useful colours can be obtained for about $44 from P.E. English Inc, PO Box 380, Thornburg, VA 22565, USA. Tel: 1 703 582 2200.)

Respecting traditions

Mark says he doesn't want to make a phoney or fake duck, or an anachronism; he respects the old traditions but wants to make a real decoy

that is part of his cultural heritage. 'I can't make totem poles, or Zulu rattles; they are not my tribe. The decoy is the cultural tool of the white North American hunter-gatherer.'

When I interviewed him in 1993 he was making a hunting rig of 12 birds for a client. His first commission was for 100 broadbills, which was when he really learnt to use a hatchet. Now he usually makes birds in pairs, but each one ends up different. He can spend time doing more complicated pieces that interest him

He approaches carving as an art form because that's how he was introduced to it, and that is his motivation to stay with it

because everything sells. He once designed a hunting box with compartments full of shore-birds with dovetailed heads. It contained shot, powder and reloading equipment. There were many requests for it, but he didn't repeat it because he doesn't work that way.

'I'm making a decoy because it is an inspiration and when I'm through with it I'm ready to relinquish it. Putting life into decoys is a sort of magic. To me it's the alchemy involved in the transition and I get the double satisfaction of passing it on to someone who obviously appreciates it. Seeing your bird in someone's home – if that doesn't make it all worth while then I don't know what does.' ∎

Fine wavy lines on the wings are created by drawing a metal comb through a top layer of grey paint to reveal the black underneath. In the green area, feather shapes are indicated by just pulling a pointed object through the paint

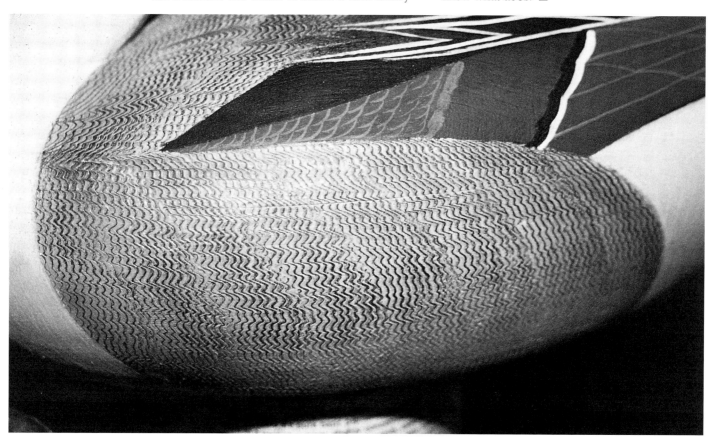

CITY
CARVING

ROBERT KOENIG

A wind felled Turkey oak was the chance that allowed the creation of Metropolis.

Robert Koenig is a sculptor living and working in Milton Keynes. He graduated from the Slade School of Art in London in 1978. Since then he has been working around the country on commissions and residencies and has had many exhibitions in Britain and in the USA, France, and Poland. He specialises in wood, but works also in stone and metal. His ancestry is Polish and he had a keen interest in Central European Folk carving.

His commissions include large circular doors carved in deep relief with images of birds, fish, acorns and interwoven branches, for St. Mary's hospital HIV and drug counselling centre in Kettering, Northants. His work has been featured in the national press and on television. He is currently working on a 14ft 4270mm high fallen cedar, with a diameter of 5' 1525mm. This will have two realistically carved 12in high figures, one male and one female.

The giant Turkey oak (*Quercus cerris*) was uprooted by the gales of 1989 in a garden in Little Linford just outside Milton Keynes. The top part of the tree was lying in a small lake. Normally single trees get cut up and thrown away, as they are too uneconomic to collect and transport to a sawmill. I am particularly interested in the large ones as they make wonderful sculptural projects. I do much of my large outdoor sculpture in Milton Keynes, so news of any large fallen trees always filters through to me. The crown of the tree was cut up on site, which left me with 44ft 13.5m of the main trunk. This was dragged out of the water and transported a few miles down the road to an arts workshop in the city.

Turkey oak has an uneven grain, and shrinks and warps unduly when planted in Britain, hence it has little practical use, although it is highly esteemed in Turkey. Here it is often planted as an ornamental tree. This particular one grew straight and very tall, with a diameter at the base of approximately 36in 900mm. It weighed about 8 tonnes.

The trunk was laid on the ground with the top end raised slightly on to another shorter tree trunk. During the course of the project the oak would be rolled over a little at a time with the help of a tractor. This slightly elevated height gave a more comfortable working position. I estimated that to keep 44ft of carved tree upright I needed about 10ft 3m of the base to go into the ground.

My idea was to carve a mass of roughly hewn, life size human figures clambering to the top, all with pained and dramatic expressions, with mouths open. It is a continuation of an idea I first had with *Rustic Dance*, a group of five wood figures carved and sited in the Ironbridge Gorge in

Rustic Dance carved in 1986 at Ironbridge Gorge, Shropshire, these five figures preceded *Metropolis* whose figures are stylistically similar

Shropshire, in 1986. The new figures were to be stylistically the same, but telling a different story. They are figures that belong to the earth, or to a passage in Stravinsky's *Rite of Spring*, or to the legends of the great fire festivals of the druids in ancient times, who are said to have made colossal images of wickerwork or wood, filled with live men and animals, then burned them in sacrifice.

The tree was carved during four months in 1991. Starting 12ft 3660mm from the base and working my way up, the figures were carved to overlap each other. Every inch of the tree was covered with bodies.

The tools used were a Stihl 024 16in petrol chainsaw, three types of mallet: a 3in 75mm lignum one for the smaller gouges and work on the detail of the faces, a 3½in 88mm lignum one for the general work, and a heavy duty 5in 127mm apple mallet that was made for me. I used a 1½in 38mm firmer chisel made by Stanley with the blue plastic handles for most of the blocking out work and a lot of the general shaping. This plastic handle was indestructable. I first tried a set of firmer chisels with the red plastic handles but they heated up very quickly and soon disintegrated.

The wood had a twisting convoluted grain, with many 'hard spots' where the grain was particularly tightly coiled. If you don't control the blows of the mallet on these areas a chisel could easily snap in half; this

Metropolis, a
column of people.
The figures
leaning out of the
column formed
from branches

has happened to me in the past. During the course of the carving I found a few nails and other bits of ancient ironwork deep in the tree. You can sometimes detect the presence of such unwelcome material, because the iron stains the wood blue in the immediate area.

A tree can often carry evidence of the past in this way. In a recent project I have found bullets dating back to the Second World War. This is one of the reasons I use a firmer chisel for the general work. I don't mind them getting damaged as much. They are easier to sharpen or replace compared to the more delicate gouges. During the four months of work I snapped two large chisels and shattered a number of wooden handles, which is about average for this size of project.

Working on *Metropolis*, the trunk supported to lift it to a comfortable working height

I use a chainsaw to cut in the outline of each figure to a depth of about 4in 100mm, then started shaping the figures with the chisels. A lot of wood can be removed by cutting across the grain at 3in 75mm intervals, then chopping out those sections with the chisel; a bit like cutting tenons. This is especially easy with oak with its medullary rays, the bright very narrow bands that radiate from the heart of the tree.

The tree had only been down for about 18 months, so it was still green. The sap stained the steel chisels a wonderful blue. It also meant that the wood was going to be

The top of *Metropolis*, the outstretched arms of the top figure carved from forking branches

easier to carve than seasoned oak, which can be very hard work. Although the main trunk was quite straight, some of the upper limbs that had been previously removed still had about a foot protruding off the vertical. This pleased me, as it allowed some figures to 'hang off' the main trunk, thus giving a more interesting sculptural effect. At the top of the tree the branches started to fork out. This allowed me to finish the column with a single figure with raised and outstretched arms. It was a satisfactory way of ending this 'endless column'.

Throughout the carving it was important to make sure that no pockets were created where rainwater could collect and rot the wood. It was designed so that the weather would run off it. I used a number of gouges for the detail work. These were:

Henry Taylor No. 9 1in
Henry Taylor No. 6 ¾in
Ashley Isles No. 5 1¼in
Ashley Isles No. 9 1¼in

The figures were quickly and roughly carved with all the chisel marks remaining. This gave a shimmering effect to the whole tree. Carving the tree trunk outdoors meant I met many people from around the world, some who had seen the Maori totems in New Zealand and the totems on Vancouver Island. I call my carving a column not a totem. It belongs to a different sculptural tradition.

The base of the column was covered in bitumen paint and sunk into 10ft 3050mm of concrete in Campbell Park in Central Milton Keynes in the autumn of 1991. The column has been titled *Metropolis* ∎

LOUDER THAN WORDS

For Dorsey James woodcarving is a visual language, his true means of self-expression. Here he reflects on the aesthetic and practical aspects of his work

Carving provides me with the silent communion with self that is necessary for me to function and grow. It is not a form of instant gratification: like most artistic pursuits it takes time, patience and dedication. At the same time, however, it stimulates and relaxes the mind.

Woodcarving is very much a fine art to me. It is a means of self-expression, a language that enables me to say what needs to be said. The words and sentences are visual and take the form of projection, recession, size, form, space, mass, volume, texture, line, penetration and degree of abstraction – not to mention the type of wood used and the subject matter.

Seeing woodcarving as a fine art demands that I approach each piece from an emotional standpoint. In other words, a greater emphasis is placed on how I feel about the piece being carved than the initial visualised image, which is subject to much change from conception to completion.

This might seem limiting but in fact is creatively quite liberating. It enables me to respond to every unexpected occurrence in the material as it is being carved. How well the occurrence reflects the initial impetus to accomplish the piece will determine whether it will be retained, altered or eliminated. I can re-articulate the form, as I carve, to accommodate very positive occurrences in the wood such as an unexpected colour or grain pattern change, or something very negative such as rot, a check or a foreign object. The image is manoeuvred mentally to include or exclude these surprise characteristics.

I know that to many this approach will seem difficult if not impossible to master – and at first it is. But with time and practice it becomes second nature and brings out the creative best in you.

A good exercise to develop this technique is simply to begin carving a piece with absolutely no idea of what you are going to

Dorsey James, now a Canadian citizen, was born and raised in Philadelphia, Pennsylvania. After serving four years in the US Air Force as a jet aircraft mechanic, he emigrated to Toronto, Canada, and worked for the De Havilland and Douglas aircraft companies.
A vocational aptitude test indicated a much suppressed but highly developed sense of creativity. Dorsey successfully pursued a five-year honours programme in Visual Arts and Education at York University. Gallery Danielli, a prestigious Toronto gallery, discovered Dorsey's work at his first student show. It has been in great demand ever since.
He has exhibited works in the USA and Germany as well as across Canada, while maintaining a full-time teaching post with the York Region Board of Education.

Samson, a biblical hero famed for his strength. Black walnut on marble base, 36 x 24in, 915 x 610mm

The face of his wife Delilah is carved into the back of the Samson sculpture

An English mythological creature, the Unicorn. Black walnut on marble base, 56 x 18½in, 1420 x 472mm

create. Draw nothing on the wood. Cut in lines, spaces and shapes that you feel suit your true mood and self. Despite the initial insecurity that you will unquestionably feel, the sculpture will ultimately define and refine itself.

Each of my wood sculptures begins with a myth or legend. I usually identify with a particular character or situation within the story which prompts me to express my perception. This generates a notion of an abstract shape that not only seeks to avoid obvious shortcomings in the material, but also creates a sense of movement, flow and/or continuity around and through the piece consistent with my own emotional imagery. The arrangement of the 'visual word' components – such as form, size, line and texture – that will ultimately tell the story, is at this point ambiguous at best.

'A good exercise is simply to begin carving a piece with absolutely no idea of what you are going to create'

Actual carving starts with the touch of the chainsaw on the material to establish the preliminary form, volume and direction. I use a 12A Makita electrical saw with a 12in, 305mm bar. I have removed the bar guard so that I can carve with the tip. It spins at 1600 revolutions per minute (RPM), so I wear protective clothing as well as eye, head and ear protection. The advantage is that I can use the saw pretty well to draw in three dimensions.

Rough form is achieved quickly and effortlessly. This is important to me because I find that wood sculpture is downright ugly ninety percent of the time you're working on it. Day in and day out, despite your efforts, the piece seems to manifest precious little of the beauty of which you know it's capable. Only in the very last stages does the work show indications that it's really happening, that everything is going to be fine. The increased speed of rendition helps to get me through the 'stock removal doldrums'.

The next level deals with coarse

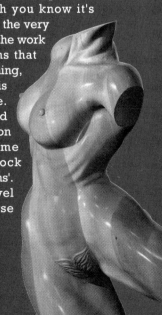

Terpsichore, Greek muse of the dance. Laminated maple, 51 x 25in, 1295 x 635mm

detailing, for which I use a Craftsman, 28,000 RPM, ¼in drive portable die grinder. This tool is most useful for creating secondary detail, surface contouring and sculpting. The portability and speed of the die grinder makes for quick and easy work on the rough hewn surfacing left by the chainsaw. It also gives enough control to see what is happening with the material by way of grain pattern and colour changes. This is where much of the subtle beauty of wood is uncovered, discovered and recovered. For me this phase is not only interesting but also tremendous fun.

Next comes the fine detailing. This is done partly with the Dremel Moto-flex grinder and partly with the Dremel Series 396. These tools bridge the transition from the ¼in drive cutters to the ⅛in drive (and less) and the fine detailing capabilities they provide. For super-fine detailing, my dentist provides me with as many 1⁄16in drive cutters and stones as I need, (this also ensures that I'll come in for my check-ups).

> ## 'I regard technology not as a threat but as an extension of my own will to reflect, accomplish and create'

Both Dremel grinders are used to create the variety of textures on the sculptures by changing the cutter type, size, angle, speed and contours, along with the size, proximity and degree of penetration of the cuts. The quantity and degree of refinement of texture should reflect the overall character of the sculpture. I find it useful to carve sample textures on a scrap of the same wood before applying it to the piece.

Once all the carving is finished, the most tiresome and tedious phase begins, sanding. I use drum sanders and sleeves on both Dremel grinders as well as on the Craftsman die grinder for coarse sanding. My wife, however, presented me with a Craftsman electric finger file for my last birthday so recently I've been using it for coarse sanding more than the grinders. It handles most of the very organic contouring with great ease.

Inevitably, though, the power tools must fall by the wayside to be replaced by sandpaper and elbow grease. Though I see no way to get around this, there are some helpful tips. Hand-made contour rasps and rifflers are ideal for levelling out those inaccessible contours. The Sandvik hand wedges and sanding belts are a godsend for crisping up edges and rim-like effects.

Another item I've found helpful is the wool-bodied, rubber-pimpled sanding glove.

Ravens from Nordic mythology, Hunen and Munen, representing Thought and Memory. Black walnut on a marble base, 18 x 12in, 460 x 305mm

Eden Seed is inspired by the bible story in the Book of Genesis. Black walnut, 17 x 15in, 430 x 380mm

It can be used during most of the hand sanding except in extremely tight situations where it tends to get in the way. However, the pound of skin it saves makes it well worth the investment. The piece is taken through sandpaper grades 50 to 600 (wet/dry).

A protective finish is then applied. I use Benjamin Moor's satin urethane cut with lacquer thinner. This immediately brings out the beautiful colour and grain of the wood, and the effect is often quite stunning. Initial application is with a fine brush. Excess is wiped off and the process is continued with a soft cloth; material from tee-shirts or from baby sheets works well. The piece may require anything from three to five light coats of this finish. Extra fine, 600 grit sanding is performed between coats. The final surface protects the piece but gives the appearance of having only been waxed.

This type of protective finish is necessary for my sculptures as they are often on public display. Frequent touching can have very negative effects on unprotected wood sculpture. The piece can, of course, just be waxed but the effect would be purely cosmetic, ie, a waxy feel and smell, rather than protective.

My sculptures sell well. I believe this is because no two pieces are alike even though I regularly repeat certain subjects. Clients often express appreciation for that fourth dimension, the story behind the piece. The story or character is usually of such a universal nature that it touches the life of the client – past, present, or possible, maybe hoped for, future. They also enjoy telling the story to friends and visitors, and pointing out hidden imagery in the sculpture.

There are those who feel that woodcarving is threatened by the onset of technology and so cling to the tried and true ways of old. That's OK because woodcarving should be what we need it to be. It must take us to that place of solitude where self-reflection can happen and self-satisfaction can blossom.

I choose to see woodcarving as a fine art and, as such, reflective of my self and my life experiences. Also, being very much a product of the twentieth century, I need to see a reasonable degree of accomplishment for my time and efforts. The power tools help me to reflect while I accomplish. And having regularly used high-speed die grinders as an aircraft mechanic in the airforce, the power tools are indeed a true reflection of my life experiences.

I therefore regard technology not as a threat but as an extension of my own will to reflect, accomplish and create. It's not the tool that is important but how it is used. St Francis of Assisi put it best when he wrote: 'He who works with his hands is a labourer. He who works with his hands and his head is a craftsman. He who works with his hands and his head and his heart is an artist.' ∎

The Greek god Pan in pursuit of Syrinx, a nymph who was changed into a reed to escape him. From the reed he fashioned his panpipes

Ray Gonzalez has been a woodcarver for over 25 years. He worked initially in the antique trade in London, learning all aspects of ornamental carving, restoration and reproduction.

Subsequently he joined MGM film studios where he worked on science fiction films such as '2001: A Space Odyssey', war dramas and historical epics. The wide range of modelling and sculptural work this involved, helped him, he says, to become increasingly versatile and to develop commercial modelling techniques.

Ray now runs his own studio in Chard, Somerset, in partnership with his brother-in-law and former apprentice Ben Harms. In addition to commissioned work, he sculpts and exhibits his own individual works such as 'The Apparition'.

He is interested, he says, in pushing back the frontiers of woodcarving while maintaining the sound disciplines of the art.

THE APPARITION
RAY GONZALEZ

An account by the sculptor himself of how the carving featured on our cover was conceived and executed.

A cabaret dancer leaping out at me from the pages of the National Geographic was the inspiration for 'The Apparition'. One of a group of dancers featured in an article about the Kremlin, her physique struck me immediately. The pose caught by the camera is almost exactly that captured by the carving.

The dancer's presence conjured up a scene in my mind of a storm-lashed cliff top on which a mystical figure suddenly appears before an unwary traveller. She may be benign or malevolent; whether she helps or harms, depends on the heart of the wayfarer. She is a storm diva.

Mentally surveying the scene, I made a note of what would be needed to bring it to life. The figure, I felt, would have to be bold and powerful, yet

otherwise separately made of metal or modelled and cast, but never carved out of solid to fit the figure. It was an extravagance I thought was justified. So that the contrast was obvious, it would have to be a different wood. With the volume of wood that was necessary, it would in any event have to be a timber more readily available in large dimensions than English walnut, which was the choice for the figure itself. But how to go about carving the cape?

The original idea was sketched to give an impression of what I was after. A larger drawing was then made and refined. Because anatomy is a life-long study, I see each figure as an opportunity to learn more — always with the aid of a live model. My daughter did most of the model work used as reference for this piece, but I also drew on knowledge of other models. There was also considerable interpretation. On other projects I have used co-workers, a mirror, magazines, the dog down the road — in fact, anyone or anything at hand that could be frozen

alluring and feminine. To convey an impression of storm conditions, the hair would need to be streaming in the wind. For the body to appear lashed with rain a hard dark timber would be needed, one which, when finished, would produce hard pool-like reflections. And to bring the scene still more vividly to life, I realised I would have to carve or select a base appropriate to the location. But this consideration I left until later with, as will be seen, results that were both good and bad.

Masochistic

At this stage it occurred to me that if the figure wore a cape that billowed in the wind, this would further help to evoke the stormy atmosphere I had in mind. Once the idea struck me, I couldn't leave it alone. The fact that I had never seen this done in wood before made the challenge obsessive. The will to find a way became masochistic.

I have seen figures with drapery that formed an integral part of the sculpted material, or

'APPARITION' INITIAL IDEA. SKETCH.

- THE APPARITION — (2nd draw.)

with a camera, or which would sit still long enough to be drawn.

Clay Model

After the drawings and photographs, a clay model was made to familiarise myself with the body in the chosen attitude, and for three-dimensional reference. A model is not always a good thing, as some pieces need a freshness of approach, dictated or influenced only by the limitations and features of the wood. Slavish copying is not advised, for clay exhibits a different spirit from that of wood, and this must be respected. However, even a direct approach into the timber is usually undertaken with a mental picture or model. So the artist is still making reference to an

archetype, however vague this may be. There is another reason for the model in this case, and that is, the cape.

Once the model of the figure was complete, it was left to dry out leather hard and then given two coats of shellac. This sealed the model and inhibited the drying process. It also allowed me to model the cape using plaster and scrim, and work out a design that could be removed from the rest of the figure and treated separately. The initial design of the raggedy cape looked all right from the front but was just a large uninteresting mass viewed from the back, with all the figure hidden. The eventual design allowed a dramatic front view and substantial areas of the figure exposed at the back. It is not a practical cape but the whole concept is fanciful, so I allowed myself artistic licence.

The process of modelling is something readers are either familiar with or not. For those who are, there is no need for in-depth description at this point. For those who are not, perhaps we may deal with this aspect of the work in detail in a future issue.

The selection of the timber was to be from English walnut and English limewood. The walnut was obtained from Yandles in Somerset and the lime was taken from a stock of butts obtained during the storms we had a few years ago. The use of storm wood was pure coincidence.

The Figure

The carving of the figure was carried out using first a bandsaw, then woodcarving gouges and chisels. The finer modelling was done with flexi-drive router and burrs. The face was sculpted almost exclusively with a hand-held motorised tool. The hair was done in a similar fashion and finished off with carving tools. The open sections of the figure were smoothed with motorised abrasives and finished by hand, using 6 grades of paper. Details were emphasised or made sharp with carving tools, and re-papered. The hands and feet were finely carved with small carving tools and finished with fine abrasive papers.

The Cape

The carving of the cape was much more complex. A block of wood 24" (610mm) long had to be cut from a trunk with a diameter of 18" (460mm) to enable the squared log to be of ample proportions. This was done with a chain-saw, and was a two-handed job. The wood was green and so the block weighed about 40-50 kilos. Even at this stage there was much waste, as the log had imperfections which needed to be avoided.

The plaster model was measured and the very bulky waste removed with a chain-saw. The inside was carved first, using an angle grinder and cutting disc. Then I used hand-held routers, carving tools and mallet to shape the inside. This was the biggest headache, as there had to be constant reference to the plaster model, with innumerable measurements with a home-made depth gauge to ensure accuracy.

When the shape seemed close to the model, the figure was fitted into the wood and constantly modified to make a perfect fit. The figure was chalked at the back and set in. Wood was removed where chalk was deposited. This was done over and over again until the fit was snug. The rest of the inside of the cape was then modelled to show the folds of drapery suggested by the model.

At this stage I decided not to finish the face since modifications might be needed. The back of the cape was another problem. After removing the bulk of the waste as before, the decision to turn it over and start removing wood from the back was taken. This is when doubts as to whether the cape was a good idea started to overwhelm. 'Now I know why I'd never seen it done, it's a stupid idea! All this work, a week spent on the cape, and now it still doesn't look possible. Should I cut my losses and just finish the figure?'

To change my mind halfway through a project is not unknown but on such occasions it is usually because I can see some improvement to be gained. In this case, it was simply defeatism; fear of failure. I could live with failure but lost time, pursuing a folly — is that justifiable? I was caught, for if I didn't finish the cape I would have thrown away a week's work and would never have known for sure whether the project was possible. I **had** to try. Besides, the figure looked unfinished on its own and I had to do something about that, anyway.

I drilled holes in strategic places using a purpose-made pair of calipers which would measure the thickness of timber at any given point. Using this guide, I drilled a vast number of holes allowing ⅜"-½" (10mm-12mm) of material. The waste in between was removed with an angle grinder for speed and then wth routers as I approached the guide depths.

The next stage was done with a mini-router and abrasive burrs while holding the cape in one hand and grinding with the other. The tears in the cape were intentional, though their shapes were modified as material got thinner, and one or two slips occurred. These tears were cut all the way through and served as further guides to the thickness of the material in various places. All the work at this stage required constant checking for thickness, and the greatest care in removal of material. The calipers used now were the index finger and thumb. I have found these to be the most sensitive instruments for constant versatile application.

> 'Once the idea of the cape struck me, I couldn't leave it alone. The fact that I had never seen this done in wood before made the challenge obsessive. The will to find a way became masochistic.'

When the shell-like cape was nearly complete, it was refitted to the figure for adjustments. The wood had shrunk and so required modification. In addition, there was some twist. To rectify this condition, the wood had to be re-wetted and clamped into position with rubber bands and string and left to dry out.

Finishing

The finishing of the figure was not much of a problem; it was simply French polished. But the cape was another question. To achieve a fine finish, it required support and this seemed impossible as it was now down to between ¼" and ¹⁄₁₆" (6mm and 1.5mm) in places. After much deliberation, the idea came to me to use expanding polyurethene spray foam.

I first placed clingfilm on the back face of the cape. This served two functions. It protected the wood from the foam and also acted as an effective release agent. The cape was placed on a board and foam sprayed between the cape and the board. When left to expand and harden, it formed a cradle the exact negative shape of the cape, one which was solid enough to enable considerable pressure to be exerted on the inside of the cape for finishing. This process was repeated for the other face, both sides of the cape being worked on alternately through the processes, including that of polishing.

Certain sections were left bare of polish so that these spots could accept resin adhesive to bind figure and cape together.

Base

The next stage was to set the carving on a base. Several crystal bases were tried but none seemed adequate. This is why, as I said earlier, the decision to leave the choice until later on was both a good and a bad one. Good planning is to choose the base and then carve the model to fit it exactly. Otherwise carve an appropriate base to fit the carving. As the choice of crystals is limited, I should have chosen the crystal first, as I was set on using a crystal base.

Fortunately there were some crystals tucked away in a room above the crystal shop and I decided to try them out. The good thing is that the one chosen had a look of the sea about it. It seemed to fit. Had I chosen one earlier we would not have searched the upstairs room. It was a last minute thing. The final choice was good for colour and size but did not sit well. The whole bottom had to be re-ground to sit properly, and this had to be done professionally. Fortunately, I am friendly with the proprietors of the little business which deals in crystals and they performed the necessary operation. My thanks to Opie Gems.

The crystal is English fluorite and is found in the Durham district. All the materials, then, are indigenous to Great Britain. If one may place any importance on this coincidence, it may be said that the figure has a Celtic pedigree. The colour and shape of the body however may suggest a more exotic location, but I feel the idea to be universal.

The crystal base was drilled to permit two steel rods to be resined in place. The lower legs were similarly drilled so that the figure could be mounted securely.

The base of the crystal could damage a polished surface so the bottom had to be felted. But this looked unfinished, so a plinth was designed to take the crystal. This was done in Art Nouveau style: flat enough not to intrude on the rest of the design while adding to the finish in its own way. The plinth was then polished and the crystal set into it with resin.

The silverwork was done partly by a silversmith and partly by myself. It added a finishing touch to the whole and provided a striking contrast to the dark walnut. At last, the carving was complete.

Despite the difficulties it has been a fulfilling experience to work on this piece. But, having done one, I shan't do another storm diva. This is a one-off. My next project will have to be something much simpler.

Unless, of course, I give myself a challenge I can't refuse. ∎

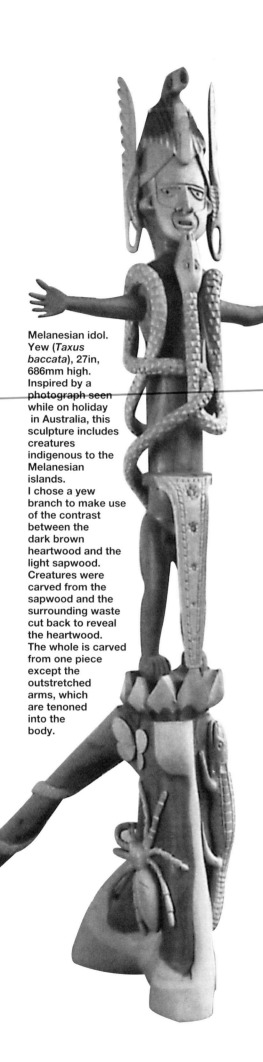

Melanesian idol. Yew (*Taxus baccata*), 27in, 686mm high. Inspired by a photograph seen while on holiday in Australia, this sculpture includes creatures indigenous to the Melanesian islands.
I chose a yew branch to make use of the contrast between the dark brown heartwood and the light sapwood. Creatures were carved from the sapwood and the surrounding waste cut back to reveal the heartwood. The whole is carved from one piece except the outstretched arms, which are tenoned into the body.

SPICE OF LIFE

Variety of style and subject matter is the key to Stan Kimm's passion for carving

When I was about four years old, I first realised that wood could be shaped with a knife. I carved a 'dagger' and proudly took it with me to school, only to have it confiscated by the teacher. From there I moved on to biplanes copied from cigarette cards, with wooden fuselages and cardboard wings, a model galleon, fretwork, rabbit hutches and all sorts of models.

I still have, and use, some of the tools I bought when I was nine or ten. They came from Woolworths when everything cost either three pence or six pence.

My father was a keen woodworker, and he taught me a lot, as did woodwork lessons at school.

By profession I was an aircraft production engineer, but carried on with furniture making, marquetry and model making in my spare time.

Some 20 years ago I took up pure woodcarving seriously, and find it completely irresistible. Subjects and styles are so diverse that I can't wait to tackle something different. I usually work on several pieces at once, and try to avoid repetition. Rarely have I had to make more than one version of any item. In E.J. Tangerman's words, I feel that I am 'a carver who marches to his own drum'.

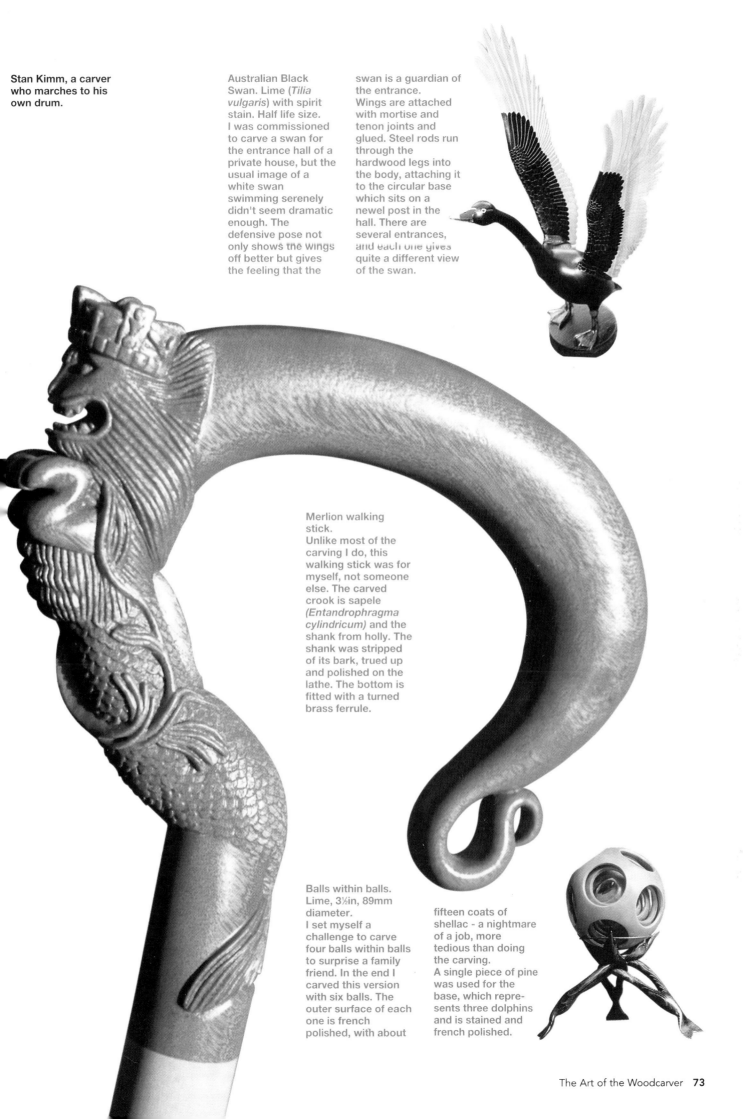

Stan Kimm, a carver who marches to his own drum.

Australian Black Swan. Lime (*Tilia vulgaris*) with spirit stain. Half life size.
I was commissioned to carve a swan for the entrance hall of a private house, but the usual image of a white swan swimming serenely didn't seem dramatic enough. The defensive pose not only shows the wings off better but gives the feeling that the swan is a guardian of the entrance. Wings are attached with mortise and tenon joints and glued. Steel rods run through the hardwood legs into the body, attaching it to the circular base which sits on a newel post in the hall. There are several entrances, and each one gives quite a different view of the swan.

Merlion walking stick.
Unlike most of the carving I do, this walking stick was for myself, not someone else. The carved crook is sapele *(Entandrophragma cylindricum)* and the shank from holly. The shank was stripped of its bark, trued up and polished on the lathe. The bottom is fitted with a turned brass ferrule.

Balls within balls. Lime, 3½in, 89mm diameter.
I set myself a challenge to carve four balls within balls to surprise a family friend. In the end I carved this version with six balls. The outer surface of each one is french polished, with about fifteen coats of shellac - a nightmare of a job, more tedious than doing the carving.
A single piece of pine was used for the base, which represents three dolphins and is stained and french polished.

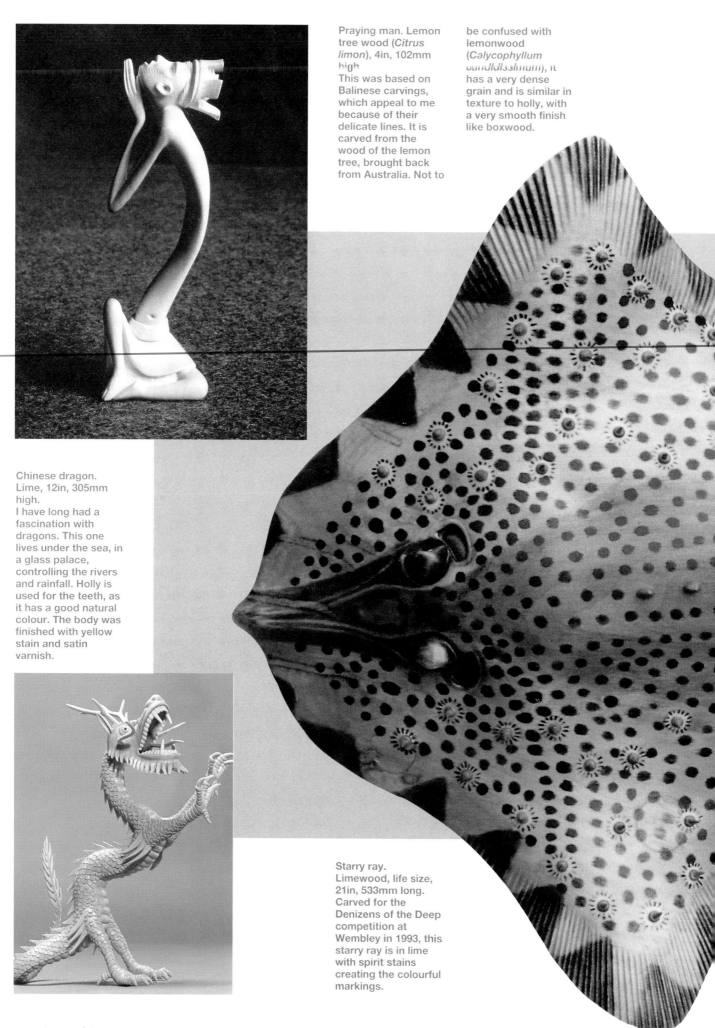

Praying man. Lemon tree wood (*Citrus limon*), 4in, 102mm high.
This was based on Balinese carvings, which appeal to me because of their delicate lines. It is carved from the wood of the lemon tree, brought back from Australia. Not to be confused with lemonwood (*Calycophyllum candidissimum*), it has a very dense grain and is similar in texture to holly, with a very smooth finish like boxwood.

Chinese dragon. Lime, 12in, 305mm high.
I have long had a fascination with dragons. This one lives under the sea, in a glass palace, controlling the rivers and rainfall. Holly is used for the teeth, as it has a good natural colour. The body was finished with yellow stain and satin varnish.

Starry ray. Limewood, life size, 21in, 533mm long. Carved for the Denizens of the Deep competition at Wembley in 1993, this starry ray is in lime with spirit stains creating the colourful markings.

Kells Beast. Mukwa (*Pterocarpus angolensis*) with limewood base. The idea for this came from an illustration in the Book of Kells. It was just a single line outline but seemed to be full of life. When in Zambia I mentioned I would like to obtain a piece of mukwa, a rich reddish brown wood, as some of the local carvers had told me it was one of their best carving woods. They said it was quite scarce, so I was pleased to be given a piece as a present just before I left. The limewood base is carved from a solid block and the whole finished with satin varnish.

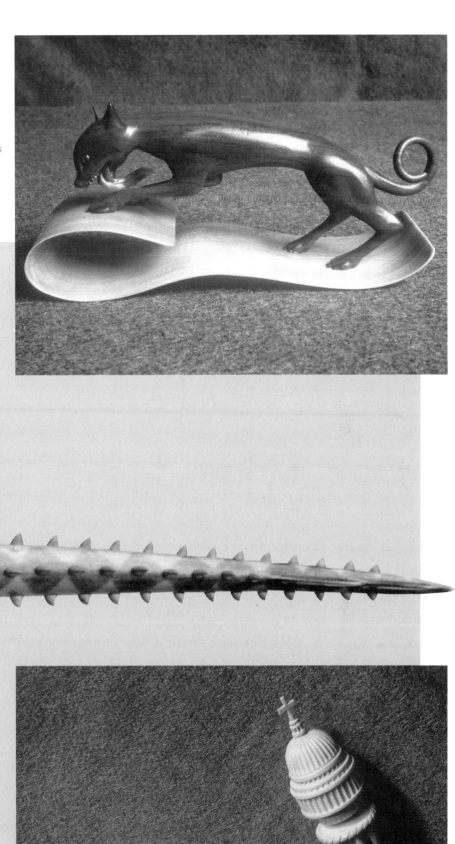

Charles and Diana commemorative wedding spoon. Lime, 17in, 432mm long. Created from one block of wood, this incorporates the wedding ring with wedding bells, the prince's crown and Prince of Wales feathers, a fertility symbol of balls in a cage, a heart made from lucky horse-shoes, the initials C and D and the dome of St Paul's Cathedral.

Eva Boyd **r**ecently **r**eturned to her native roots having spent 26 years in rural Essex.

She now lives at Haltern, in Germany.

Eva enjoys writing about woodworkers and woodworking. She is a regular contributor to the *Ruhr Nachrichten* at Haltern.

Her articles and features have been published in newspapers and magazines in Germany, England and Hong Kong – about art, restoration, cookery and travel. She also published two cookery booklets in aid of charity.

THE GLORY OF GOTHIC

Sacred themes, her homeland and the German Gothic tradition inspire the work of Gertrud Büscher-Eilert, as Eva Boyd discovered

Gertrud Büscher-Eilert's artistic career started early. As soon as the four-year-old farmer's daughter could hold a pencil she started drawing. Not the things she saw — they held no interest for her — but those things in her head that were struggling to get out. She still recalls the clarity of those early images of fairy-tale figures and religious motifs.

Before she discovered the possibilities of wood, she experimented unsuccessfully with loam and marl stone. But once she had got hold of a simple little knife, the 11-year-old girl was transforming wooden clogs into nifty little boats and carving whimsical Punch and Judy figures. Small commissions for carvings came from the local church.

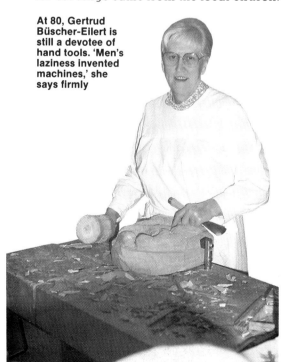

At 80, Gertrud Büscher-Eilert is still a devotee of hand tools. 'Men's laziness invented machines,' she says firmly

All photographs by A. Westerdick

Her major work, the Wettringer winged altar. Carved in limewood and coloured with oil paints, the scene shows St Peter sinking into the Sea of Galilee after having doubted Jesus

Although her father and the local priest recognised her budding talent, Gertrud's mother tried to prepare her daughter, the seventh of ten children, for the role of traditional farmer's wife, and sent her to a college run by nuns. Soon she was carving figures for the church nativity scene while the nuns supplied bits of embroidery to reassure her mother that Gertrud's education was progressing nicely.

Breadless art

Eventually her mother resigned herself to the fact that her daughter was going to pursue 'breadless' art and Gertrud attended Münster Arts & Crafts School (1938-1940) and from 1941-1942 the renowned Folkwangschule at Essen Werden. It was only after the war that she started her own business.

In the quiet of her home tucked away in the countryside of North-West Germany, Gertrud talks about her work. 'The main focus of my work lies in the depiction of religious themes. It does not lead you to believe in a perfect world or a superficially beautiful world, nor does it show a world marred by reproach, disunity or resignation. Through my art I address man in all his complexity, not merely his intellect. In my work I never exaggerate.'

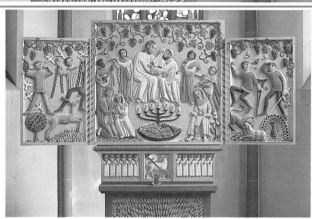

The wings open twice to reveal two more narrative pictures: here of Christ's resurrection. Strong simple shapes and flowing lines give movement to the composition

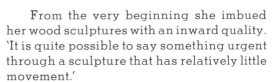

Second scene from the altar — 'God will wipe away all the tears'. Gertrud follows in the tradition of Gothic folk art, drawing inspiration from the rural, domestic details of life around her

From the very beginning she imbued her wood sculptures with an inward quality. 'It is quite possible to say something urgent through a sculpture that has relatively little movement.'

Composition is very important. 'A relief, a sculpture, must be alive, have movement, but be careful not to cut out its soul by "overworking" it. Hundertwasser, the great Austrian graphic artist, said quite rightly: "All straight lines are ungodly." But remember, before one can express movement, one has to work for quite a while in a closed style, whether your medium is wood, clay or stone. If you don't, too much detail is going to blur the message you are trying to get across.'

Hands on

'Wood sculpting is not a question of sheer physical strength but of technique,' she says. 'It is the way you hold and handle the wood.' Working without drawings, without using clay or plasticine models, demands her total concentration. Only for reliefs does she make a drawing.

Machinery is an anathema to Gertrud. 'Men's laziness invented machines... These are my favourite tools,' she says, pointing to a handful of English-made pre-war gouges. The makers' names are almost worn away but I can just make out Newring Bros and Merry Bros, imported by Otto Lichtmann, Berlin. 'The well-hardened, beautiful thin steel can be sharpened with ease and I use these gouges on the details of every face I sculpt and on large figures, too.'

In the early days, her favourite brother used to fell trees for her. Since his death during the war, Gertrud's wood supply comes from a local forest warden. Sometimes she manages to get hold of solid oak beams from old houses and timber from disused windmills.

Although she favours German oak for its strength and because it is 'the carver's wood', used both in Germany and England by medieval craftsmen, Gertrud also likes linden wood (limewood) because it is light, neither too hard nor too soft, and can take fine detail and sweeping forms. Also its close grain allows cross-cutting.

'During the Middle Ages,' she explains, 'linden wood was fairly abundant throughout Germany which is why most late Gothic reliefs were carved from it.'

Honest folk

Gertrud always disliked Nazarene work, a style created in the early 19th century by a circle of German-Roman artists; it struck her as kitsch and false. In contrast, Gothic carvings and wood sculptures were an important early influence. 'Maybe because they represent true folk art. They have a wealth of beauty, expression and form because ordinary people helped shape their development.'

Gothic carvers and sculptors made extensive use of colour, using watercolours with egg, gum or glue as a binding agent. 'In Bavaria they go for colour in such a big way that an unpainted sculpture is known as a "blind saint",' says Gertrud. She also uses watercolours but mixes them with a wax stain when a sculpture demands a soft tint. Otherwise she chooses acrylic, which is more resistant to light, or occasionally oil paint, as for the Wettringer winged altar, to make the bright hues stand out.

However, she does not try to copy the typical colours of Gothic carvings. 'I use my own designs for which I choose colours that suit the present.' Paint seems to give a sculpture softer contours and heightens the three-dimensional effect; swathes of drapery catch both light and shadow. And, she says, used properly, colours can emphasise or even change an expression.

Craftsmanship

Her major work, the Wettringer winged altar, took four years to complete and entailed lengthy consultation, different design ideas and drawings.

Apart from the oak shrine, which was made by a renowned local carpenter, all other work was undertaken by Gertrud herself. The wings open twice to reveal three different narrative pictures. It takes some time to study the detail and appreciate the pure craftsmanship. The altar seems to overshadow the architecture, which becomes nothing more than a backdrop.

One of her most important sculptures is *The Tree of Life* which tells Jesus' message (Matthew 10,39) in six scenes, arranged under the branches of a tree.

A local carpenter hacked off large bits of the 2m, 6ft high linden tree until the rough outline of the sculpture emerged. To avoid cracking and to reduce the trunk's considerable weight, Gertrud hollowed it out at the back. Then she went to work on it with a woodcarving mallet and large carving chisels, after drawing a rough sketch of her design with a piece of charcoal. As the low relief progressed, she used smaller gouges and knives, finally stabbing and chipping away with a knife in each hand.

Gertrud has spent nearly all her life in the same place, and draws her inspiration from it and its people. So when she sculpts a tree it is always a Westphalian tree she has in mind, and when she carves the image of someone to convey an idea, it is based on a real person. Their faces are earthy and their shape exudes dignity and strength — physical and mental. The limewood madonna in her studio, despite grand swathes of drapery, reveals feet that are anything but dainty. Standing firm, they declare they have not left this earth — not yet anyway.

Although Gertrud has never courted personal publicity, her work is renowned throughout Germany and has been taken as far as Mexico by some priests.

Some of her experience gathered over a lifetime has been passed to her adopted son Erich, now aged 31, who, like her, discovered his fascination for wood at the age of 11. Although his talent is already widely recognised, by giving him her name she hopes he will find it easier to establish himself. ∎

The Tree of Life, carved in limewood, 2m, 6ft high, tells the story from St Matthew's Gospel. It was hollowed out at the back to reduce the weight

Detail of *The Tree of Life* showing the return of the prodigal son. Only a rough charcoal sketch was done before carving directly into the piece

Griffon, English walnut, 12½in, 315mm wide. My first ever carving!

DRAWN TO CARVING

Ray Winder describes how, though trained as a graphic artist, he was attracted to woodcarving

Ray Winder was born in 1953 in Surrey where he still lives and works. Married with two young daughters, he has been a professional artist for 20 years, working as a freelance illustrator mainly for advertising agencies and design groups. The move to carved wood as a medium has presented him with new challenges, and he continues to experiment to further his own personal development.

Ray would like to see woodcarving gain a higher profile generally, and to see it taken seriously as a form of sculptural art as well as a relaxing and creative pastime.

Ray's work has won many awards and is in private collections in the UK, Brunei, the USA and Luxembourg. He has had several articles published in the woodworking press and was recently elected Chairman of the British Woodcarvers Association.

I have been attracted to wood since my schooldays, when woodwork came a close second to art as my favourite subject. My love of painting and drawing was so strong that, despite not knowing what future there would be in it, I persuaded my parents to let me go to art college (well actually my art master did!). I attended a degree course at Kingston in Surrey and, after the first year, specialised in graphic design for three years.

By the final year I was back to painting and drawing as I could see I was destined for commercial illustration. I left college with a BA in the summer of 1974. Within a couple of weeks I had found an agent to represent me and suddenly I was a 'professional' artist. This was the start of a whole new learning process. I was expected to produce highly finished illustrations of any subject, on demand, at very short notice and usually with tight deadlines. I learnt fast!

This was my life until about five years ago when I stumbled across woodcarving. I'd thought about working in three dimensions many times but never got around to it. Once introduced to carving I became obsessed with it and wondered why I'd not discovered it earlier. I soon acquired the 12 carving tools I thought I would need, and of course a mallet.

It seemed a natural step from working in two dimensions to start with a relief carving. I decided on a mythological creature, the Griffon. None of the pictures I could find fitted my idea of it, so I prepared my own pencil drawing. I spent a lot of time on this first carving as I was at the beginning of another new learning curve.

After completing a few carvings, I realised that carved wood could be used as a form of illustration. I began showing my work around, and had a certain amount of success, although reaching the right people in an industry badly hit by the recession was not easy. I have recently been accepted by one of London's leading artists' agents who will promote my carved work to advertisers and publishers.

Some of this work could be classed as modelmaking in wood. It's still carving but the ideas can be supplied by someone else, and I have to make them work. It's good discipline to work accurately without any leeway for altering or 'improving' a design to suit my own tastes. It helped me to master the tools and make them do exactly what I wanted.

Finding suitable pieces of wood at short notice can be a problem. I work in native or occasionally North American hardwoods, and my experience of woodyards is that their definitions of 'well air-dried' are variable. With care, splitting and checking has not been a problem, although this does depend on the size, and choosing the right species for the job. However, warping of relief panels can occur overnight, even with the driest wood, if large amounts are removed rapidly and not enough time is allowed to let the wood stabilise. I keep a moisture meter close to hand, which gives me an indication of when problems are likely to happen.

> **'It's good discipline to work accurately without any leeway for altering or improving a design to suit my own tastes.'**

I have not added many chisels to the dozen I started with. These are Swiss Pfeil brand and I have always been happy with them, although I also have some from Bristol Design and Ashley Iles. Most will get some use at one time or another, but I often use the half-a-dozen favourites rather than stop to find something of a more suitable size or profile.

I now rely heavily on an angle-grinder fitted with either an Arbortech disc or a powergouge disc for roughing out. The brutal efficiency of these cutters saves a lot of

Leonardo, lime, 15in, 380mm high.

This was my second carving. I had been told that limewood could be carved into fine detail with a smooth finish, and I wanted to explore these qualities for myself. I chose the self-portrait of Leonardo da Vinci in order to combine his features in very shallow relief with the high relief of curly parchment.

It was carved from a 3in, 75mm thick block of wood; the edges of the paper were carved very thinly with deep undercutting to make the effect convincing. The finished carving was mounted in a deep frame as it is very fragile. Now in the collection of The Honourable John Fermor-Hesketh.

Horse Head, painted lime, 20in, 510mm high.

Although we all know the shape of a horse's head, few are familiar with all the bumps, depressions, veins, hair directions and so on. A horse's head is as individual as a human one, so I photographed one animal to work from. It was not a difficult carving, but burning all the hairs into the wood was rather time consuming.

I coloured the head using thin acrylic paints, the eyes were also carved and painted but finished with gloss varnish to give a 'wet' look.

precious time but they must always be treated with respect. Heavy gauntlets and eye protection help to shield against those stinging chips.

I will use any tool if it speeds up routine waste removal, from an electric chainsaw to small burrs and scalpel blades. As my background is in art and design and I have had no formal woodcarving training, I don't feel restrained by traditional methods and attitudes to carving and believe the end justifies the means.

One of the most important things I keep is a sketchbook where I scribble down all the ideas that come in to my head. These may be developed at a later date into something more finished.

I'm greatly attracted to simple shapes and forms in wood, particularly if unusual

Acorns, English oak and painted limewood, 16in, 405mm high.

This piece was commissioned as a brochure cover for a printing company called the Acorn Press. The butterfly, a purple emperor, is another image the company use because it is indigenous to the Hampshire oak woodlands where they are based. The block of oak used was 3in, 75mm thick and the butterfly was carved larger than life size from lime and then painted using acrylic paints, with metallic powders added to give an iridescent sheen.

Zephyr, English walnut, 17in, 430mm high.

A zephyr is a west wind and I decided to carve a head with an intense windswept look. I first made a clay face to get the features right and added cardboard wings to calculate the size of the block of wood.

The head is made from two pieces; the collar was carved separately and joined to an elongated neck afterwards. The face and wing section came from a large block of recently felled wood and was quite wet. There was some distortion of the wings as the wood slowly dried, but fortunately it is barely noticeable.

textures or natural flaws can be introduced or utilised. I would like to explore this more in the future for my personal work. I feel some carvers try too hard with elaborate displays of technical wizardry, which don't always work, when a simpler but more carefully thought out and refined design might have more appeal. Grinling Gibbons was not only a brilliant carver technically, he also had a rare gift for composing all those fiddly elements so that they just looked right, which is a very difficult thing to do.

I think drawing is very important. It's not essential to make elaborate studies for a carving but a few quick sketches will often help. Drawing can help you understand the

subject and become aware of the difficult areas that will need most care to carve. Having said this, most carvers are hobby carvers, who haven't the time to practise drawing or are not that serious. For them, copying others' work or drawings is the obvious answer. They will still have to observe carefully, and so will be exercising visual skills without perhaps realising it.

In the future I would like to explore new outlets such as galleries, and to develop some high profile commercial projects. Not just to make a living, but to give more widespread exposure to carved wood, so that it can be seen not only as a hobby but also as a visual art to be taken seriously.

Dreams Carried on Golden Wings, English walnut, bleached lime and 9ct gold, 16in, 405mm high.
This carving became a companion to *Zephyr* and they were later bought as a pair. I wanted to create a serene dreamy look, emulating Art Deco bronze and ivory figurines, without of course using animal ivory. I used lime for the face and bleached it just before it was 'inlaid' into the head. The winged headband motif was carved from jewellers wax and cast by a specialist in 9ct gold.

Environmental Care Award, approx 22in, 560mm high.

I enjoyed this job as I had a free hand to do my own designs. The trophy is awarded to the South East of England council that has done most for the environment that year. It was sponsored by British Gas who were keen to get away from the typical piece of engraved glass. I wanted to combine elements that symbolised growth and renewed hope for the environment. A large walnut pod with oak leaves and acorns curls open to reveal a smaller pod of yew, which in turn is splitting open with a white shoot in sycamore sprouting up. This nestles in a piece of yew root that was sandblasted and then cut and polished to reveal a deep rich area of rot and that lovely swirly grain. In keeping with the nature of the award, all the woods came from storm-damaged trees.

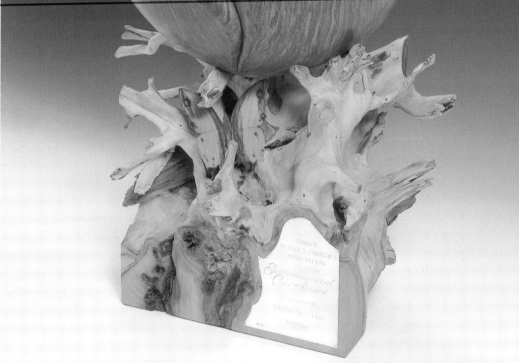

Pledge Can, olive ash, 18in, 460mm high.

This was a recent advertising commission, for Johnson's Wax, of an aerosol can emerging out of the background. I chose a 4in, 100mm thick piece of ash, with darker olive streaks running through the heart, for its colour and anticipated final appearance rather than its carving qualities.

A cardboard template was used to check and maintain the curve of the cylinder shape as the carving continued. The lettering was carefully marked on the wood and cut using scalpels and mini-burrs. The finished carving was stained to give a richer colour, emphasised by the photography.

Jaguar XJ220. One of my most recent carvings, this was also one of the most demanding to produce. It is a one-sixth scale 'model' of this stunning sculptural supercar, and required a block of English walnut 32in long, 14in wide and 8in thick, 813 x 355 x 203mm. The wood was quite wet when I started and I drilled the underside extensively to remove waste wood and relieve drying stresses.

I had the full co-operation of Jaguar Sports Ltd and made several trips to the factory to photograph and measure the real cars. The difficult part was interpreting the flow of the curves from the photographs. Glossy paintwork can be attractive but it doesn't always show the real shape underneath.

Shortly after completion, the carving was bought for the collection of XJ220s owned by a member of a Royal Family in the Far East.

VAULTING REVIVAL

Les Jewell has restored many vaulted screens including a rather special one in Blackawton's church

V aulted screens are found in many churches in West Country England, with a great many of them here in Devon. The earliest wooden screen of this style dates from somewhere in the late 14th century to the middle of the 15th. The vaulting on these screens has a practical purpose in that it forms a walkway over the top of the screen. As the vaulting projects about 36in, 900mm each side, the total width of the walkway is about 6ft, 1.8m – access to the walkway is usually by a short flight of steps inside the thickness of the church wall.

Above **At one time these screens were painted, on this one with numerous repairs and misguided cleaning, most of the colour has disappeared**

Over the years age and death-watch beetles have caused a large amount of damage to these screens and I have helped to repair many of them. While engaged in work on the screens I have been able to recognise the work of individual carvers from the past. I assume that a band of itinerant craftsmen went from church to church, probably staying on the site as some of the churches are quite remote, even today. No record is left of the names of the carvers and joiners who made these screens. Only their work remains as their monument.

Symbolic division

All the screens are made in English oak and they extend right across the width of the church. Sometimes called chancel screens or rood screens, they separate the nave of

The screen was a sorry sight.... It was obviously going to be a big job

Top left **Many rood figure have disappeared, Les Jewell has carved several replacement sets**

Above left **Detail of the Mary figure, Christ is supposed to have just said, 'Woman, behold thy son.'**

Above **The screen from Blackawton church before restoration**

Right **A rare example of a screen that has retained its original colour**

the church, where the congregation sit, from the choir, where the clergy and choristers conduct the services.

You can see that the work wasn't skimped by the way that the backs of the screens were also elaborately carved. The back faced the choir and sanctuary, the most revered and holy part of the church. In folklore it is said that the idea was that the simple peasantry looked through the perforated screen from the cold dark nave into the brightly lit choir. With its brilliant paint and gold leaf, they had a glimpse of paradise – almost unattainable.

The purpose of the walkway on the top of the vaulted screens becomes clear when you find one with the rood intact (rood is Old English for cross). The rood, which may have started as a simple decorative cross, now comprises three figures: Christ on the cross, Mary the Blessed Virgin and John the beloved disciple in attendance. This group, high above the screen, emphasised the reverence of the sanctuary. The walkway on the screen gave access to the rood, for cleaning and maintenance. I have been told that the sacraments were sometimes stored by the rood for safety – the door at the bottom or top of the steps would, of course, be secured.

Blackawton restoration

Blackawton is in the South Hams, in Devon. The parish was totally evacuated of civilians during the Second World War, and given to the US Army to be used for training for the invasion of Normandy. As the training was to be under realistic battle conditions, it was anticipated that much damage would occur, so the church, amongst other buildings, was shut, boarded up and all moveable furniture taken away and stored, including the church screen.

Although Blackawton's church has a 'Gothic' vaulted screen, the style of carving on the screen is completely different. Built in Tudor times (16th century) it has the initials of King Henry VIII and Catherine of Aragon carved on it. It is clear that its style is transitional, leading on to the later Jacobean style.

It was not until the early 1960s that the decision was made to re-erect the screen. A generous grant from the Pilgrim Trust enabled work to be started. When it was unpacked from its case, and temporarily set up in the workshop, the screen was a sorry sight. It was shorn of its vaulting, with only a few fragments of the carved panels left. It was obviously going to be a big job.

First came the joiners, who erected the vaulting - this is a work of art in itself. The ribs of the vaulting, when put together resemble the spokes of an umbrella. I have spoken of the skills of joiners before and, when you see how they incorporated small fragments of the original screen into the new panels, their skill is clear. The old parts were set into the triangular vaulting panels before the panels were carved, presenting the joiners with a real challenge.

Another particularly difficult area was the running ornament above the vaulting. The joiners had to butt the repairs tightly to the old wood, and leave enough material for us to carve in new decoration. It is to the credit of the joiners and their work that this could be successfully completed. As you can imagine, the carving of the new pieces to harmonise into such a fragile surround demands great care.

By studying the old fragments of the screen I was able to design the new panels to represent what I am reasonably sure was their original state. Then my apprentice and I were able to complete the carving. I did not try to reproduce the medieval painting, it is something I have never done. The repair is there for all to see.

The carved panels on the intersections of the vaulting were more or less intact, and can be seen in all their glory, with all the medieval paintwork intact. A boss is a square piece of decorative carving with the function of covering the joints where the vault ribs meet. On one of these I carved what has become my 'trade mark' a thrush. It is not acceptable to sign your name on church work, nevertheless, features such as the carver's favourite bird or animal are a clear signature to others in the know.

Links with the past

The lowest part of any church screen is usually in contact with a stone floor. This makes this area prone to rot, and the Blackawton screen was no exception. The bottom sill had to be replaced and so did most of the tracery panels. In a previous article in Woodcarving I mentioned that a pattern called Aaron's rod was much beloved by medieval carvers. In Blackawton church it can be clearly seen on the original piece of the transom that was put back during the restoration.

Some paintings are visible on the bottom panels of the screen, but I don't know if these are original. Many were destroyed during the Reformation and these could be later replacements.

The completed and assembled screen gives great satisfaction to those who worked on it. We are happy in the knowledge that the reconstruction was done step by step, in the same way that it was built all those years ago. It had to be done by hand, in the same manner as old, or the whole appearance would have been ruined.

So we maintain our link with the past. As some of my tools, and some of the joiner's as well, are well over one hundred years old, they have been used by generations of craftsmen. It may be that the link is unbroken.●

With its brilliant
paint and gold
leaf, they had
a glimpse
of paradise

Left **A boss with Les Jewell's 'signature decoration', a thrush**

Top **Restored vaulting at Blackawton church – a masterly display of joinery and carving**

Above left **The pomegranates in the restored panels are said to be part of the arms of Catherine of Aragon**

Above right **The sill and tracery panels had to be replaced due to rot, the paintings are old but of uncertain date**

LARGE

I n December 1986 a wooden block was delivered to Armand LaMontagne's studio. It measured 84 x 40 x 30in, 2130 x 1015 x 760mm, and weighed nearly a ton. It was to become the portrait of basketball player Larry Bird.

Dave Cowans, director of the New England Sports Museum of Boston, and former player and coach for the Boston Celtics, wanted a large sculpture for the museum. Larry Bird was his first choice. According to LaMontagne, 'Bird was sceptical about the project. He asked why now, why not later or after he had died. My answer was that it makes it easier for me to do the sculpture. It makes it more accurate. You'll look better; I'll look better. It's the ideal way to do it.'

Magic wood

The block is basswood (*Tilia americana*), laminated in 4in layers, which is LaMontagne's favourite wood for carving. 'Basswood lends itself to making what you want. It's hard enough that once you cut it, it holds detail. Yet it's soft enough to carve without problems....An extremely hard wood fights you all the way. I take the wood and, like a magician, change it to something else – sneakers, pants, hair, eyes.'

Before cutting into the block, LaMontagne stocked his studio with a variety of reference materials. On easels were two life-size watercolour portraits of the athlete. The uniform hung in a corner, with a pair of his size 14 sneakers. A pingpong ball with an eye drawn on it rested on a workbench. And a National Basketball Association ball was propped up on an empty coffee tin.

ARMAND LAMONTAGNE IS RENOWNED FOR HIS REALISTIC LIFE-SIZE PORTRAITS (SEE LAST ISSUE). HERE HE TALKS TO ROGER SCHROEDER ABOUT THE RE-CREATION OF BASKETBALL STAR LARRY BIRD

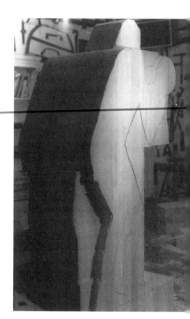

Mental block

LaMontagne likens himself to a runner. 'Runners reach the wall,' he says, 'but I reach the block. It looks like a mental block, but therein lies the challenge. I have to do this, no one else can do it, and that's when the excitement starts. That block kindles my spirits.'

Armand LaMontagne in his well equipped workshop
Above right
Profiles were drawn on paper and transferred to the block as a guide for roughing out
Right
Reference material included full-size watercolour portraits

First step was to hoist the block upright. He nailed a piece of carpet on the floor where the block would rest, so that it could be moved more easily. Then using a hook attached to a massive ceiling beam, and a block and tackle, he brought the wood to its full height.

To create patterns for roughing

AS LIFE

out, LaMontagne did not use the painted portraits because they had been drawn in perspective and so would produce a distorted figure in three dimensions. Instead, patterns were designed separately on paper, perforated along the pencil lines, taped to the block and powdered with chalk to leave a line on the wood.

Moving mountains

Once the patterns were transferred, he began to remove the waste wood with a chainsaw. According to LaMontagne, this is the most challenging part of sculpting any large figure. 'In the initial chainsawing, I'm taking some very drastic steps, moving mountains immediately in the process of subtractive sculpture. I'm taking a lot of risks, and this requires as much or more skill as any other part of the process. And you have to be very accurate early on. I have something to lose since things happen fast, but they are calculated to happen that way. I try to get the largest amount of excess off in the fastest way I can.'

In only one day he can begin to see how the sculpture is developing. Using a mallet and chisel is not only too slow but also 'the safe way to sculpt. And I never take the safe way.'

Multi-function chainsaw

In fact the chainsaw is many tools in one – bandsaw, gouge, and he even uses it as a rasp. To avoid taking off too much wood as the figure begins to be defined, he holds the blade perpendicular to the surface and chips away small amounts of wood.

Chainsawing can take several weeks on a piece this size. Since

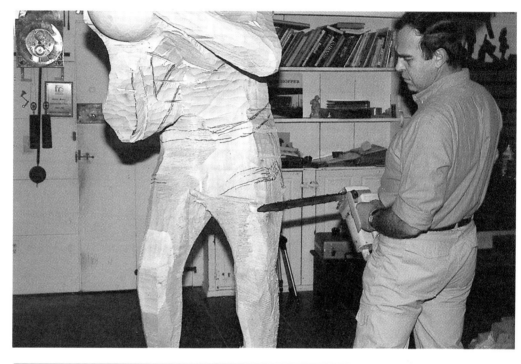

IN THE INITIAL CHAINSAWING I'M TAKING A LOT OF RISKS, AND THIS REQUIRES AS MUCH OR MORE SKILL AS ANY OTHER PART OF THE PROCESS

Much of the early shaping was done with the tip of the chainsaw

Sculpting began with the ball. A simple cardboard template was used to check curves

the blade is only 14in long, it is not possible to cut from one side of the block to the other. Consequently, small pieces of the block come off, leaving profiles of different thicknesses. Where the chainsaw can't be manoeuvred safely without risking overcutting, LaMontagne uses a large boring bit, which can take out a plug of wood 3in in diameter.

On the ball

After the basic shape had emerged from the block, LaMontagne did not start refining the body or even touch the head. Instead, sculpting

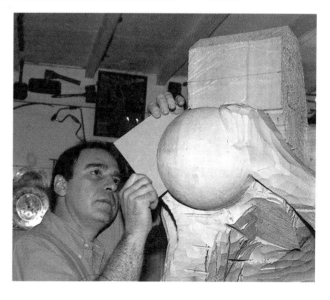

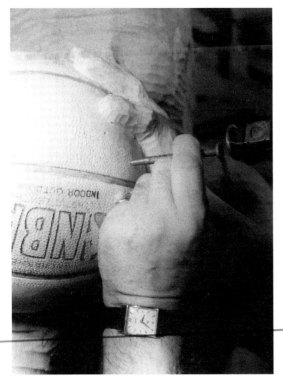

A good deal of time is spent on the face: 'The hardest thing was getting the sculpture to look like Larry Bird. I spent half the time on his face. And I do that on every sculpture.' When it came to the final refining of the head, using full-size photographs for reference, he used small gouges, pushing them with his hands to remove slivers of wood – time-consuming but precise.

Despite his dismissive attitude to details, LaMontagne is meticulous in reproducing them. On the face he used what looks like an ice pick to put in pores and the flat of the same tool to impress wrinkles. Eyes are not glass but painted wood, finished with many coats of a high-gloss polyurethane. 'You can go to a taxidermy shop and buy bird eyes,' says LaMontagne, 'but you can't buy *Larry Bird* eyes.'

He spent hours laying out the knit of the socks, and many more hours putting in the repetitive details with a home-made stamp. Another home-made stamp with the reverse pattern filed into the steel was used for the knit of the shoe-laces.

Above
Punching in the rubber pimples on the ball

Above right
Many carving problems were posed by the proximity of the ball to the face

Right
To create the repetitive pattern on the socks, a pattern was filed into a piece of steel, which was then used as a punch

THE BALL WAS THE PIVOTAL THING. I STARTED THE BALL AND PLACED LARRY BIRD AROUND IT. IN EFFECT, BIRD BECAME THE SECONDARY FACTOR

began with the basketball. He says it was 'the pivotal thing...I had to be on the ball. It had to be perfectly spherical, precisely in the right place. I started the ball and placed Larry Bird around it. In effect, Bird became the secondary factor in the carving.'

There was also a practical consideration, as LaMontagne explains: 'If I did not complete the ball first, that would have left me less room to carve the face. I had to take as much wood away as I could from in front of the face since the ball is so close to it. And I needed every eighth of an inch to be able to work.'

This basketball is exactly the same size as a real one. Callipers and a simple cardboard template were used to check dimensions and curves. The rounding was done with gouges and chisels. To create the raised rubber 'pimples', LaMontagne used a metal punch and pounded it into the surface.

Once the ball was complete, the body was shaped with large gouges and a mallet, and the tip of the chainsaw.

There was a problem with the arms, however. Both arms were sharply crooked at the elbow, making them vulnerable to damage while the sculpture was being worked on. The solution was to leave extra wood around the right elbow joint and to brace the left arm by leaving an extension of wood connecting the chest to an area just below the wrist.

'I create solutions with each statue,' says LaMontagne, 'and I never do the same thing twice. Or if I do, it's by accident, not design. I'll know what to do when I get there – just get me there. It's called experience. The details come later. I worry about the basic pose: the rest just follows. If I'm off on the basic pose, I have nothing. No amount of details will correct a basic error in composition. That's a fundamental law.'

Having established the pose, and using accurate measurements taken from the real Larry Bird, slowly and proportionately, the sculpture lost weight.

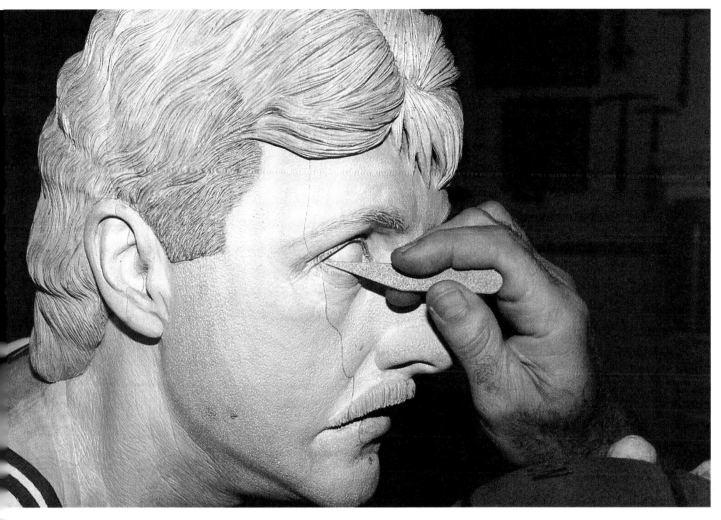

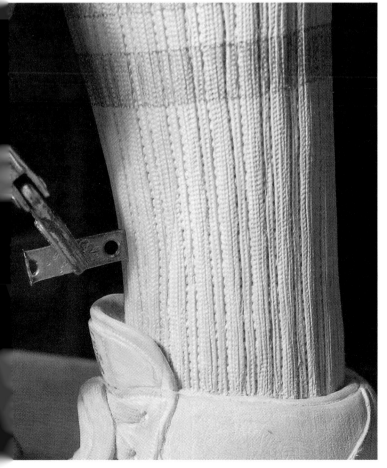

Improvisation: an emery board cut to a point is used for fine sanding in tight corners

Left
Hand-made punch used to reproduce the pattern on shoelaces

Below
One of these shoes was carved; the other is the real thing

Customised tools

Although LaMontagne's worksho has an impressive array of tools, h is constantly improvising. If fo example a gouge cannot remov wood from a tight corner, he take the temper out of it and bends it t the shape required. For fine sandin he uses an emery board, which ca be cut to a fine point for even th most inaccessible places. When came to the emblem on Larry Bird uniform, to create the slightl coarser material he applied a heavi coat of paint and textured that.

For the base, LaMontagn decided to put the statue on piece of the Boston Garden floo which is made of red oak. Rath than cut away the figure an insert new wood, he used what h jokingly calls 'the thinnest vene possible'. He copied the floor b painting it on to the basswoo base. No one has been able to te that it is not real oak.

Final reaction

Six months and a couple thousand hours later, the statu was completed. When Larry Bi saw the finished work he wa astonished at how much resembled him. LaMontagne wa also taken aback because in th meanwhile Bird had had a unusually short new haircut. S he decided to do the same to th sculpture.

Asked if he sees any room f improvement on the wor LaMontagne says that his stat of baseball star Carl Yastrzems is technically a better piece, 'if f no other reason than it came aft Bird. My standards get higher every one. In the scheme of thing Bird may be an average piece.' ∎

Terry Martin was born in Melbourne in 1947. A graduate of Armidale College, Adelaide, and the University of New England, New South Wales, he has had a satisfying and adventurous life travelling the world in various capacities, including Stage Manager of the Royal Opera House, Covent Garden, Ski Patrol in Austria, geological exploration in the Pacific Islands and Migrant Education in Australia.

A growing appreciation of fine craft work was heightened by several years spent in Japan and when Terry returned to Australia he decided to pursue his interest in woodcraft.

Terry believes that woodturning allows use of limited timber resources for maximum effect. Much of the wood he uses is recycled, such as fence posts or railway sleepers. Influenced by Japanese ceramics and other crafts, he believes that the natural faults of the timber should be allowed to remain to enhance the work he does on the wood.

WOODCARVING IN JAPAN

TERRY MARTIN

Our Australian correspondent, lately returned from Japan, reports on the woodcarving scene there.

A pair of fierce dragons

Japan is an ancient wood culture. Despite its massive consumption of imported hardwoods in modern times, it has always valued its own indigenous timbers as one of the few natural resources the country possesses.

Because Japan is so earthquake prone, building was usually done in wood — a material that is more likely to flex during tremors than rigid stone or brick structures. Among the oldest of these wooden buildings are the shrines of the indigenous Japanese religion, Shinto. The timber used for the most prized of these buildings has been *Hinoki*, or Japanese Cypress. An alternative is *Keyaki*, or Zelkova. These timbers are easy to work and contain natural oils that keep the wood in good condition for centuries, although they are often left unfinished. They are usually allowed to weather to a light grey colour. The shrines are often highly decorated on the outside and covered in intricate carvings.

Yoshiichi Yokoya at work

Concentration

Religious Shrines

On a recent trip to Japan I took the time to visit some of these shrines on the Izu peninsula, about 150 kilometres south-west of Tokyo. It is a peaceful area with an air of ancient history. The shrines are common and appear unexpectedly — tucked away in neat compounds creating havens from the hustle of Japanese life.

On entering a shrine one passes between two guardian lions carved in stone (Photo 1). The inner precinct of the shrine is considered extremely holy and the work done on the building by the craftsmen was particularly significant.

A first glance under the eaves of a shrine will reveal an incredible array of intricate carving (Photo 2). Some of this carving is merely decorative and enhances the structural members of the building (Photo 3). But the majority is more representational and shows a whole menagerie of fanciful dragons, lions and other fearsome denizens of the spirit/animal world. There are birds, turtles, elephants and huge, foaming waves swirling around the pillars, with the whole entwined in foliage covered in delicate blossoms and insects.

Young Japanese still visit these shrines on special occasions, but the significance of the religion has declined. I saw a few very sad examples of decaying shrines and the only really new one I saw was made in concrete! What will happen to these buildings in the future is hard to say. There are so many of them that I don't think this beautiful carving will disappear, but whether the young people care enough for the craft to be preserved is another question. It is still possible to feel the power in the hands of the craftsmen who created these carvings and the conviction of the beliefs that inspired such art.

A Traditional Carver

Everywhere you go in Japan you are surrounded by woodcarving. It is part not only of religious images but of the architecture, theatre, and so on. So I was very interested to meet a traditional carver during my visit. His name is Yoshiichi Yokoya and he is a second generation carver from the Asakusa district of Tokyo. He was exhibiting his work at a craft show in Kawasaki and I was pleased to see that he also was demonstrating.

Mr Yokoya was hard at work when I arrived and I spent some time watching him before I introduced myself. I was intrigued to see that he was carving a figure of Buddha and that he was almost the image of a Buddha himself. If you looked quickly you could be forgiven for thinking he was a meditating monk! His concentration was intense and his work was rapid and smooth. Displayed behind him were pieces for sale, mainly religious images. Prices ranged from £40 to £5,000! He quickly finished his little Buddha and showed me the seven tools he used to make it.

The Buddha and the tools used to carve it

I asked him if I could interview him, but that proved rather more difficult. He belonged to the 'strong, silent' mould of Japanese craftsman and appeared to believe that modesty forbade talking about himself. I was able to find out that he was trained by his father in *EDO KIBORI* style (old Tokyo style carving) and took over the title of Master from him. His specialty is shrine and temple carvings and he is known for his images of Buddha. I learnt that in 1981 he was given an award for superior skill in his craft by the Japanese government. Then in 1990 he was given a special medal from the government in recognition of his work.

I noticed that there were little bags of wooden chips for sale and asked what they were for. It appears that his best carving wood is sandalwood and he sells the offcuts for people to put in their wardrobes for the scent. Each bag contained about six pieces of one inch square each. The price was about £10 per bag! I couldn't find out if this was due to the price of sandalwood or to the fact that they were offcuts from a famous master, but I did have images of shipping container loads of Camphor Laurel from my workshop in Australia at several dollars per chip. Oh well.

When I asked Mr Yokoya about his tools he said they were made by a swordsmith who was, coincidentally, exhibiting in the next room. So, after many thanks to him, I went to the next room to meet Teruyasu Fujiwara, fourth-generation swordmaker. Unlike Mr Yokoya, Mr Fujiwara's father still works, so he has yet to inherit the title of Master. He makes a great variety of blades as it is not possible to live off the limited demand for traditional swords. When I arrived he was sharpening a chef's knife (Photo 5). A lot of his work is for master chefs who each demand a different style of blade for the incredible variety of Japanese cuisine. It would have been impossible for him to demonstrate forge-work in the gallery, so I had to be content with watching him sharpen his blades. The traditional method is to work over a tub of water containing the various stones so that the tool and the stones can be constantly wet and rinsed off (Photo 6). The stones were all Japanese and he insisted that these were superior to any other kind. He also made carving tools for professionals, and I was able to buy a tiny gouge for about £25. There were swords on display and a poster in the background showed Mr Fujiwara forging a sword blade in the traditional way.

It was an unusual chance to meet two men working in related crafts. They were both obviously proud of their traditional lineage, although neither was arrogant about his skill. I could feel the calm confidence and contentment that came from being respected craftsmen in a country where such people are still highly regarded and where the future of their work seems assured. ∎

'I could feel the calm confidence and contentment that came from being respected craftsmen.'

Teruyasu Fujiwara sharpening a knife. The poster in the background shows him forging a sword

Traditional sharpening

BOY MEETS GIRL

The demise of a 200-year-old cedar tree was a golden opportunity for sculptor Robert Koenig

It was the same old story – a magnificent old tree had become dangerous and had to be felled. I heard about it from local tree surgeons who had worked on it in the past, and introduced myself to the owners. A one-off tree, no matter how grand, is usually too expensive to move and would have been cut up and burnt on the spot. I offered to take on the expense of moving it.

The tree, a 200-year-old Atlas cedar (*Cedrus atlantica*) was 5ft, 1.5m thick at the base and approximately 70ft, 21m high. Its main trunk was 20ft, 6m long and the thickness didn't change very much along that length. It was one of a pair of cedar trees planted close together on an estate near Milton Keynes in Buckinghamshire; the second tree was to benefit from the extra space and light created by its felled neighbour.

Moving tale

A large wedge had been cut out of the base as part of the felling process. I thought if the base was cut level, the large diameter would be enough for the trunk to be stood up safely. This was done using a chainsaw with a 4ft, 1220mm bar. I settled on the main 20ft length because beyond that the limbs had begun to branch out. These huge branches would have made the trunk less stable and the extra length would have added to the transportation problems.

Access to the site was difficult and the lorry needed to be big enough to pick up about 10 tons of timber, without damaging a thin asphalt driveway. (The cost of any repairs to the asphalt were down to me.) However, the risk was worth it and despite the problems the tree was delivered safely to a farm in Milton Keynes where it was to be carved.

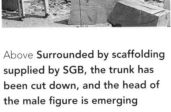

Above **Surrounded by scaffolding supplied by SGB, the trunk has been cut down, and the head of the male figure is emerging**

Below **A tooled finish was chosen to add life to the piece**

Left **Robert Koenig with his sculpture, *Boy and Girl*, Atlas cedar, 14ft, 4.3m high, 1992**

In an upright position, this huge piece of timber with its dark-coloured bark presented a frightening if impressive sight. It took some time before I got used to standing underneath it looking for inspiration.

Support services

The tree was delivered in November 1991. I spent the winter visiting it regularly and planning the project, which I started after the worst of the winter weather in March 1992.

Work had to be done outdoors as the barns on the farm were too low for the crane to stand the trunk upright. I only had short notice of the tree's imminent felling, so there wasn't time to find a more suitable indoor site.

I needed scaffolding for the project and approached a local firm, SGB, not knowing how long I would want it. They were very supportive of my idea, and erected the structure with three separate working platforms and a 20ft, 6m ladder, free of charge. Projects of this nature are often not feasible without such generosity.

Climbing to the top of the scaffolding was one thing, but working on the tree with a chainsaw was quite another, especially as I needed time to convince myself that it was indeed stable in this upright position. Initially I moved along the top platform having secured myself to the scaffolding with a harness. This changed after a week as it became impractical, and by then I had gained more confidence.

Under the skin

At the start the usual procedure is to take off the bark to see what the wood looks like underneath. Any flaws and nails or other

BOB GREEN

Left **Most of the carving work was done with a mallet and large chisels and gouges**

Below **Almost completed work, ready for colouring**

ironwork that could damage chainsaws and gouges are then revealed. I found that many limbs had grown together and trapped large pockets of bark deep inside the tree. This became more apparent at the top. Because of these many flaws I decided to cut the tree down to 14ft, 4.3m high. A chainsaw with a 3ft, 915mm bar was used to cut large blocks off the troublesome top part. These were later used for woodturning. Some offcuts ended up in various local houses for their aroma: as it was a freshly felled tree the smell of the cedarwood oil was very strong. Other offcuts were turned into disc shapes ready for relief carving; these give off a squeaky sound when rubbed. The timber has a wonderful golden honey colour.

This huge piece of timber with its dark-coloured bark presented a frightening if impressive sight

Larger than life

As I had been carving people for some time, I felt it was an ideal opportunity to carve a really large figure, as big as the tree would allow. The proportions of the timber allowed for two figures 11ft, 3.4m high on a 3ft, 900mm base. I took photographs and made drawings of a friend in her typical dress of short skirt, leggings and big boots. I also made a scale model carving in lime of a male figure, loosely based on myself, to a height of 3ft, 900mm. The drawings were scaled up, and I referred to these preparatory studies regularly on site.

The two figures were to stand upright, back to back. At this stage the most important question was where to place them on the trunk to avoid the worst of the remaining flaws still visible in the timber. They always seem to appear where you don't want them: the most visually sensitive part of a figure carving is the face, and you don't want a length of bark suddenly to appear across the cheek. I spent a good deal of time changing the position of the two heads.

Bold cuts

Once their placement was decided, I progressed steadily down from the top to the feet, working on both figures at the same time. The whole surface was handcarved and many flaws and knots, some 12in, 300mm wide and others tiny but as hard as stone, had to be negotiated. However, I broke surprisingly few gouges and relied heavily on my 1½in, 38mm Stanley firmer chisel for heavy duty blocking out work, and my Stihl 024 chainsaw. Other gouges used were the Ashley Iles alongee gouges, No.3 2in, No.6 2in and a No.9 1½in. The handles always take a pounding so I use a heavy duty tape to bind the ends, which seems to prolong their life considerably. On this job I kept a roll of tape with me to make running repairs, as my studio was four miles away.

Most of the carving was done with bold cuts from these large gouges with little attempt to conceal the marks they made. They created a mottled regular surface effect which I felt made the carving livelier. Details such as the faces and hands were carved with a variety of small gouges; again the marks they made remained. I often add colour to my figures and in this case I used a Trebitt wood protector which is available in many different colours. After eight months' work the carving was completed in the autumn of 1992.

Standing back to back, the two figures look as if they might have had a row, but not so. They are a couple and yet independent, forward-looking and confident. The carving appeared twice on television news reports, was shown at the Milton Keynes Futureworld housing exhibition and is currently back on the farm awaiting a more permanent home. ●

Robert Koenig is a sculptor living and working in Milton Keynes. Since graduating from the Slade School of Art in 1978 he has worked on commissions and residencies throughout the UK, and has exhibited in Britain, the USA, France and Poland. He specialises in wood but also works in stone and metal and has a keen interest in central European folk carving

UKRAINIAN CHIP CARVING

The traditional Ukrainian style of chip carving is preserved in the USA by Michael Korhun.

Chip carving, characterised by complex geometric designs, has been used for centuries to decorate household articles, farm implements, vehicles and architecture throughout Europe including the Ukraine. As with other forms of Ukrainian folk art, techniques and patterns were passed from parent to child for generations, so that by the 19th century Ukrainian chip carving had developed into a complex regional style.

Unfortunately, the intricacies of traditional chip carving have fallen out of use in the Ukraine. Emigrants, however, such as Michael Korhun of Troy, New York, have taken their memories and skills with them and have found support and encouragement in the many Ukrainian organisations throughout the USA.

Unlike other traditions that employ chip carving, Ukrainian carving begins with a stained and finished surface. The carver then chips away finished wood to expose the raw wood beneath. The resulting interplay of dark finished wood with light new wood is the hallmark of Ukrainian carving. With this method mistakes are not forgiving, any stray cut will show up on the stained, glossy surface. Traditional Ukrainian carving, also includes inlaying beads or stones, and has been used to create patterns on boxes, plates, bowls, and turned vases and urns. The majority of Korhun's work is the decoration of turned work.

Michael Korhun was born in Jazyny in the central Poltava region of Ukraine in 1924. His farming family, he says 'didn't have much time for the arts.' But, his father was a craftsman who made violins, so Michael was exposed to woodworking at an early age. By the time he was a teenager, Michael was carving small figures and, as a prisoner in a work camp during World War II, he found he could trade carvings to the guards for bread. After the war, he studied sculptural carving with Russian carver Arkadi Lapsenkov.

In 1952, Korhun moved to the United States with his wife Maria and settled in Troy, where he found work as a toolmaker. Although he was already proficient in sculptural and relief carving by the time he came to the States, Korhun didn't begin to explore Ukrainian chip carving until 1965. Since then he has developed his skills to make pieces that are astounding in their complexity and use of pattern.

His work is currently in demand for exhibitions throughout the northeastern United States and Canada, and he has been nominated for a National Heritage Arts Award through the National Endowment for the Arts. Korhun has recently returned from his first trip back to his homeland, the newly independent Ukraine, where his work is now on display at the Museum of Ukrainian Folk and Decorative Arts in Kiev and the Museum of Regional Studies in Poltava.

Turning

When making a vase, Korhun begins with a freshly cut green log, rough turns it inside and out, and then sets it aside to dry. Rough turning reduces the chance that the piece will split as it dries. He prefers to work with fine-grain hardwoods, such as maple or poplar, but he does not limit himself to these woods.

After the piece is turned, Korhun sands it, ending with 280-grit emery cloth. Prior to

Circles are cut with a veiner fitted to compasses

Straight lines are marked with flexible plastic strips

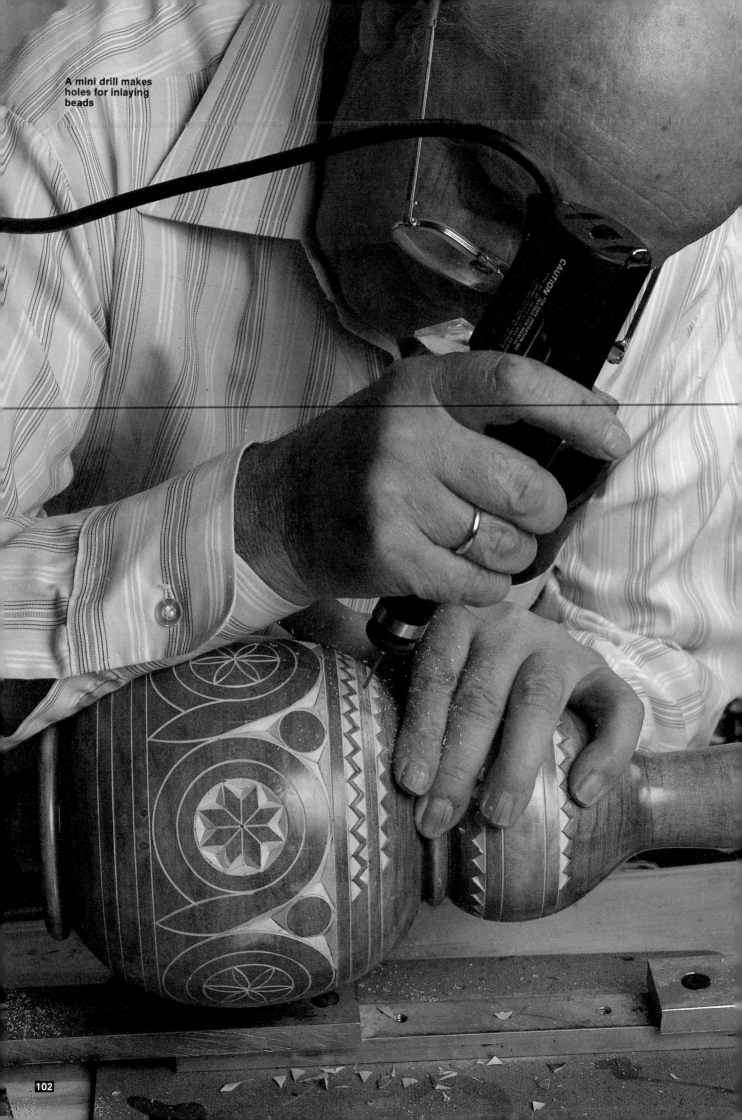

A mini drill makes holes for inlaying beads

a pair of dividers to mark centres of circular motifs. Transparent strips of plastic with parallel lines incised on them are used to lay out straight lines. Then he begins to carve.

Carving

Circles are carved with any one of a number of different sized compasses fitted with miniature veiner chisels that Korhun grinds, files, hones and polishes, so they will carve a crisp line in a single pass. After the parameters of the design are defined by incised circles and straight lines, the spaces between the lines are carved by removing triangular chips, incising lines, or stamping patterns with a variety of simple dies.

Although some chip carving, like the style associated with the Swiss, is done with a knife, Korhun uses chisels. And while his kit contains scores of different tools, he made most of them to get into the tight spots he encounters when carving in the round or in relief; chip carving only requires a few chisels. Zig-zag borders are cut in two passes: once around with a 90° v-tool to outline the shape and final pass with a straight chisel to pop out the triangular chip with a single thrust. The tools must be sharp to ensure clean cuts and to avoid wasted effort.

Other chip-carved areas, where triangular cutouts combine to form inverted pyramids and fan-like patterns, are cut in similar manner — the triangles are outlined by striking a chisel with a mallet, and then the chips are popped out with a controlled thrust by hand. To add a finishing touch and to highlight portions of the design, Korhun inlays coloured beads. The beads are simply pressed into holes that are slightly smaller than the diameter of the bead.

The importance of traditional craftsmen such as Michael Korhun should not be underestimated because they are the traditional bearers for skills which might otherwise fade away. ■

applying a finish he turns the emery cloth over and buffs the wood with the cloth backing. Then he applies four or five coats of Red Devil polyurethane varnish stain to the outside. A coloured varnish is ideal for this technique because the stain doesn't penetrate the wood. This is important because much of the effect of the carving comes from the crisp line between the finished surface and the carved areas.

It is amazing to learn that Korhun does not sketch details of the design on to the vase with a pencil, nor does he work out the patterns on paper; he designs each piece as he goes, remaining true to a few principles of Ukrainian design.

Korhun uses chisels rather than a knife for chip carving

The pattern stands out from the varnish stained surface

Marking out

Korhun divides the piece into thirds or quarters by marking each section with double incised lines. To make sure the lines are straight, the tool is held in a notch cut in a piece of aluminium tubing that fits in the toolrest bracket, and the workpiece is rotated slowly by hand. Then, using an indexing head, Korhun divides the circumference of the vase to locate centres for the circles or stars that will be the primary design elements.

Now Korhun removes the workpiece from the lathe and takes it into his basement where he has a corner set up for carving. This little carving studio is equipped with a suitcase-sized chest full of chisels and tools he's made, a frame to hold the workpiece between centres and a workbench that can be adjusted up and down with a crank just like a scissor jack.

With an idea in mind of what the main elements of the design will be, Korhun uses

HERALDIC ACHIEVEMENT

ROY BISHOP

THE HERALDIC ARMS, OR ACHIEVEMENT, WERE REQUIRED TO GO OVER THE FIREPLACE IN A SCHOOL LIBRARY.

Roy Bishop is a native of Somerset and has lived most of his life in that county and its neighbour Gloucestershire, where he now has his workshop. He was fortunate enough to have been apprenticed under excellent craftsmen at a time when traditional craftsmanship was more common. After the war when restoration of bomb damage was finished, quality work became scarce and he decided to help pass on skills to the next generation, entering education where he spent the next 25 years. Over the years he has established a reputation for traditional carving, remaking classical period pieces, and lettering. His personal interest, however, is in heraldry and nature studies which are accurate and reflect the spirit of the subject. He has a steadily growing collection which he uses to illustrate talks and raise funds for conservation. Having spent a lifetime observing nature, his sculptures endeavour to capture that fleeting moment which reflects the aura of a subject, while combining with the natural beauty of wood.

Heraldry is such an absorbing and interesting subject that in preparing this article I found myself running into pages of introduction which would have made a small book. I have therefore decided with great discipline to restrict myself to the matter of carving one piece of work. There have been many achievements made with other media, plaster, stone, marble, metal, and clay, but none can produce the depth and sharpness of those carved in wood.

Fortunately there are still people who care enough about their history to invest in keeping it alive and passing it on to the next generation. Would that many more cared similarly about the world which they inherited; hopefully they will at the eleventh hour. One such group of people is the staff, governors and parents of Prior Park Preparatory School at Cricklade in Wiltshire, led by the Headmaster John Bogie. Over the years this hard-working group has created a school environment rich in quality and tradition, to which I have been privileged to make a small contribution.

The carved and painted arms of Priory Park Preparatory School

The school arms were designed by the College of Heralds and I was commissioned to produce a carved shield for the entrance hall. This was quite large 3′ x 2′ 4″ x 2½″ 915mm x 711mm x 63mm. It is in my opinion a particularly pleasing design and deserved my best efforts. I made it in lime and every detail was carved before being painted. I was later commissioned to produce another achievement 10″ 255mm high, for a panel over the fireplace in the beautifully restored library. Being without a base, completely pierced, it presented an interesting challenge.

Draw then carve

In my opinion one cannot become a complete carver without developing an ability to draw. In the days before photocopiers we had to draw, trace and produce blueprints for each part of a large job. It was quite often a craftsman's talent in drawing which singled him out in the workshop, leading him to develop skills for certain pieces of work which meant he became a carver.

To the best of my knowledge, while guilds date back for carpenters and joiners there is no record of a guild of carvers. Of course there have been many men who spent the majority of their working life carving and sculpting, often in a variety of materials; to mention in hushed reverence but one, Grinling Gibbons. Anyway back to the job in hand, today photocopiers have been developed to such high standards that they can be enlisted to save much time drawing. Where size restrictions are involved however one still has to resort to pencil and paper.

One is usually given a small picture to work from. If you are not too strong on freehand drawing you can enlist the assistance of a pantograph or use the squared method of enlarge-ment, then make a tracing from the full-size drawing. The next step requires some thought, how thick should the wood be? Sometimes one is given limits in size, in which case the work is made to suit, but when you have the choice the depth of each part can be determined in the best interest of the subject. Using carbon paper transfer the drawing from the trace. I find a tracing useful as sometimes it's necessary to re-draw parts and tracing paper helps in re-alignment.

Modern plunge routers are of great assistance in roughing down to the first levels, but one must be alert to retaining the boundaries of each area. In this case I allowed a fraction more on thickness, not cutting to the lowest depth required. In pierced work weak parts are inevitable, so it is advisable to maintain support as long as possible. It is surprising how much strength even a veneer thickness will lend.

Waste is removed with a router first, then details are blocked out

Tool choice

In these commissions one is usually working from a painted design and it is up to you to turn that into an accurate three-dimensional interpretation. The forms are tackled usually working away from the highest part to the deepest. I'm sure there will be many interesting and scientific discussions in these pages extolling the virtues of one tool over another for different tasks, which will send enthusiasts diving for the tool catalogues. In my experience most professional carvers have a fairly small number of gouges and chisels which are regularly used, while rolls of others collected or made over the years spend most of their time 'resting'. Therefore I will recommend the tool advised to me many years ago by craftsmen who carried to their graves with them more practical knowledge

Carving is nearly finished, the lettering and other fine detail is cut after an undercoat is applied

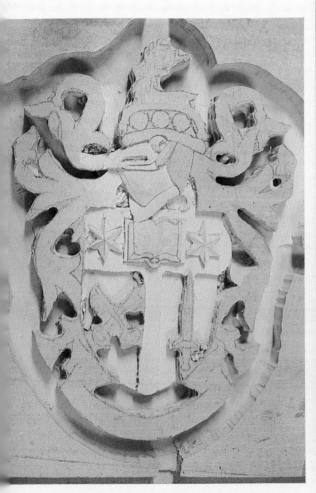

and skill than the highest qualified expert of today will ever have — use the most suitable one to hand — it's really a matter of common sense.

Far more important than the tool to use is a knowledge of how the wood will work. Remember that in three-dimensional work most parts include working with the grain, across the grain, against the grain and in end-grain. If the tool used, whatever its form, doesn't leave a smooth surface, it isn't sharp enough! In roughing out even small work like this, it is possible to use a light mallet to speed things up. Just a word of warning do remember that every cutting tool has a wedge action; if the bit you want to remain is weaker than the bit which you are trying to remove, well guess which breaks out!

I started carving down from the helmet in this case. Keeping the outlines I formed the book, stars, sword, keys and then the shield. I do not recommend detail work at this stage, just block it out in case you have to alter any depths. Next I formed down to the routed depths of the pierced parts, again don't go right through at this stage. The crest, spheres and stag were next, leaving the antlers blocked to protect this delicate area.

From now on it's hand work all

With lettering cut and a second undercoat, the painting begins

The finished arms; the depth of relief is more apparent in this view

The achievement in place on the library wall

the way; for me anyway. I know that some people use flexidrives with burrs and drills with round cutters. They certainly have their place and can save some time, but on this job not much and at what cost in noise and dust? Give me a good clean cut any day. For the mantling it's a case of thoughtful care, watching out for short grain and checking that all the parts are flowing in the correct way curving over or under as required in the drawing. With a carving on a back board the undercuts only go out of sight to meet the board, with this piece every part has to be completed, seen or not.

Now for the detail work, if you can start in the centre of a job like this it prevents one having to work over finished delicate work.

I think it helps in delicate work to think like a cricket batsman, look around the field before taking each guard, it saves having to say — 'Oh bother!', or whatever polite expression you use on a cold day when your dust coat catches in a delicate protusion; usually when the bell rings on that damned contraption designed to interrupt carvers.

When cutting forms such as the stars on this shield, check the

drawing. It may be that they are required to be slightly different, but if they are painted the same, you must make them the same. In heraldry there are so many meanings in the design, and what the College of Heraldry says, goes.

Once the head, mane, hooves etc, are formed on the stag and the waves on the spheres, leaves on the book, sword and keys, it's time to remove the support. This cuts away easily, but do be careful near the short grain bits. This achievement has to be painted, so very fine work which requires to be sharp is left until after the undercoats are applied. Items such as lettering and tassels can be cut through the undercoat. The last detail is the antlers, these are carved with support under, but I permitted myself to finish with a little glasspaper stick. The final stage is the painting. Colours are very important in heraldry, each having a special name and relationship which would take an article in itself to cover. Suffice to say that the colours in the painting have to be matched exactly, which usually means mixing. Some experience in miniature model painting is invaluable in some of the very fine parts, because it is often too small or inaccessible to mask. Just one final tip, in first class work dust can spoil a finish as it dries, so one of those transparent kitchen covers, can be useful.

That is about all there is to it really. This is not the smallest heraldic shield I've made by a long measure, but it was an interesting little challenge. ∎

HIDDEN TREASURES

Ryan Bowler discovers a cache of fine carved misericords

The parish church of St Mary's, in the English Cotswold town of Fairford, Gloucestershire, is famous for its exquisite stained-glass windows. Surrounded by such works of art it would be easy to miss other treasures from the past.

It may seem odd to find visitors on their knees peering under the choir stalls, but it is here that a rich hoard of misericords can be found. These were ledges on the undersides of the hinged seats, on which choristers could support themselves while standing during the service. They were often richly carved.

Those at St Mary's are said to date from the time of Edward I (1272-1307). It is thought they were originally made for the abbey at Cirencester about 10 miles away, and were brought to Fairford shortly after the dissolution of the abbey in 1539.

All life is here

In total there are fourteen misericords, depicting scenes from everyday life. Some

From top left clockwise
Fox and geese
Man with two dogs
Couple drinking cider
Grotesque head

show people and their relationships: a woman remonstrating with her husband; a youth teasing a girl; a man and woman sharing a cider barrel; two men still hungry; a drunkard.

Others depict people going about their chores: a woman plucking a pigeon; a man with two dogs; reapers with a wheatsheaf; a woman spinning while a dog sniffs for food.

Animals also feature prominently with carvings of a fox and geese, a hawk killing a duck, and two wyverns – heraldic beasts with wings, a serpent's tail and a dragon's head. Finally there are pictures with a symbolic meaning, such as an angel and a grotesque head.

Past masters

Although not as imposing as the stained-glass windows, the misericords have their part to play in recalling the life and times of an earlier age.

Apart from regular dusting and polishing, they have remained in their original state for 700 years, an enduring testimony to the skills of the unknown craftsmen. ■

A pine burl bowl carved by a woodworker from Atna in Norway

BURL BOWLS FROM NORWAY

MARTIN NOLTE

The inside story about sculptural vessels carved of Norwegian burl wood.

Martin Nolte lives with his family on a farm near Paderborn, in Germany. He farms 50 acres and is a member of the German organic farmers' organisation, *Bioland*. Besides, he edits the German turners' quarterly journal, Drechseln, and enjoys writing about woodworking and woodworkers.

Did you ever breakfast in a mountain hotel in Norway? Perhaps you remember the breakfast buffet: breakfast rolls served in huge burl bowls! Carving vessels from burls ('burrs' for readers in Great Britain and Ireland) is an old Scandinavian tradition. I didn't know this when I first came across these remarkable vessels while on holiday in West Norway.

For farmer/fisherman Steinar Distad, birch usually serves as firewood to heat his farmhouse, which is by the Fjaerlandsfjord. But when Steinar finds a birch burl, on a tree in the woods above the fjord, he will use his skill with the chainsaw for something less trivial: making 'natural-shaped' bowls.

I stayed in one of Steinar's beautifully restored wood chalets for three weeks, but I might never have seen his rugged sculptural vessels if I hadn't been burl-hunting myself. On a mountain walk through Steinar's land I had spotted two 10" diameter birch trees with burls growing all around the stem. On returning from the woods, I asked the farmer if I could cut some burls to take home for bowl turning. Both of us were surprised, Steinar because of my find, myself, because he immediately understood what I had in mind. Steinar generously told me to cut what I needed and invited me to his farmhouse to see some of his own carved bowls; some measure up to 20" across. He told me that he made

these bowls in winter — when daylight only lasts six hours in West Norway — a time when tourists are few and farm work is reduced to feeding the sheep in the barn.

The burls that Steinar Distad prefers are mostly root burls — the largest that birch trees offer, but the most difficult to cut if you want to leave the tree standing. The complete growth can only

Birch burl bowl by
Steinar Distad,
about 500mm
20" across

Birch burl vessel
by Steinar Distad
about 550mm
14" across

The
Fjaerlandsfjord in
West Norway

be removed by several plunging, angled cuts — 'shearing' the tree, as the sheep farmer himself likes to call the procedure. These 'shearing' cuts make it possible for Steinar to carve vessels whose outside is also the outside of the burl.

The chainsaw is also used for hollowing out — plunging cuts again — while most of the inner carving is done with a grinder attached to the power drill; leaving a wall about 1" thick. Steinar Distad leaves the outer shape just as it appears under the bark. The bark can be most easily removed in spring, when the tree is in full sap. Steinar is interested in the natural, rugged shape of the vessels, not in showing the typical burl grain, so he does without sanding and finishing.

Steinar Distad is a farmer and a part-time fisherman, and he lives in a rather remote corner of Scandinavia (he is proud of the fact that the ancestors of Walter Mondale, the former White House Spokesman, once emigrated to America from the Fjaerlandsfjord). As far as I know, Steinar has never exhibited or sold one of his vessels, though I can imagine them displayed in an art gallery. For me, his vessels are of the same beauty as the chainsaw carved burl vessels of the American artist Mark Lindquist the beauty of nature.

Long after my holidays in Norway, I discovered Mark Lindquist's book *Sculpting Wood*, which is the most informative book I know about the harvesting, turning and carving of burls. A major part of this book focuses on chainsaw carved burl vessels.

Lindquist makes most of his chainsaw carved vessels much in the same way as Steinar does: first using the chainsaw, then with a grinder attached to the power drill. As an artist who makes objects for art collectors, the American goes further with finishing. A circular disc sander is used to smooth rough surfaces and also to continue refining the form. As to the final shaping of the edge, Lindquist writes in *Sculpting Wood*: 'Although the disc works well in shaping the outer edge, additional hand tools may be employed. The Surform tool or sculptor's rasp allows for more precise control in sculpting an area. I like to fine tune an edge with a foam pad dowel.'

After shaping and rough sanding, Mark Lindquist begins the final finishing, using the flexible back foam sanding pad chucked into an electric drill. The artist sands the entire surface of the bowl through each grit: 80, 150, 220, 320. 'If carefully done', Lindquist says, 'foam back sanding can entirely eliminate hand sanding, producing a perfect finish with no swirl marks or scratches'. Lindquist's burl vessels are finished with several light coats of penetrating oils and then buffed with tripoli.

Both the Norwegian farmer and the American artist use modern power tools which eliminate hard labour and allow them to work quickly. Traditionally, Scandinavian woodworkers used (and still use) mallet and chisel, rifflers and rasps. Needless to say, the traditional procedure is a very long and tedious one, requiring not only skill but also muscles!

If you want to go the fast way — chainsaw carving — why not ask a chainsaw expert to do the dangerous part of the job for you? If you don't happen to know somebody really skilled with the chainsaw, you might just contact your local Forestry Board. ■

You can find more information about chain saw carving techniques in Mark Lindquist's book *Sculpting Wood - contemporary tools and techniques*, Worcester, Massachusetts, USA 1986.

SUPERSTAR SCULPTURES

Armand LaMontagne's sculptures of sporting heroes take realism to new heights, as Roger Schroeder describes

Roger Schroeder is a prolific writer and lecturer on woodworking, construction, sculpture and carving, as well as a cabinetmaker and amateur carver. He combines these activities with a full-time job as a high school English teacher, specialising in teaching writing and research

Portraits in wood by Armand LaMontagne are so highly detailed and realistic, they look as if they are ready to step off their pedestals. A typical example, from 1987, is of Boston Celtics player Larry Bird poised for the free throw. The carved basketball has the look of dimpled rubber; socks have a knit pattern that could deceive a tailor; the sneakers look as if they could be in a shoe commercial. No detail is too small or insignificant: the artist re-created chewed fingernails, put moles on the face, painted hair on the arms, and made a crooked little finger, the result of an old injury. It took about six months to complete.

LaMontagne's explanation for this meticulous attention to detail is simple: 'People don't want interpretations. They want to be portrayed as they are.' He compares his work to portraits in three dimensions: 'they end up being the ultimate trophy, a life-size statue in full colour.'

'Cultures are generally known for their art – architecture, paintings, sculptures, writing,' LaMontagne points out. 'My art documents outstanding individuals for the ages. And I'm continuing a tradition as old as Man.'

Every one a winner

Although he has sculpted famous Native Americans, as well as public figures such as former US President Gerald Ford, First Lady Eleanor Roosevelt and General George Patton, he prefers athletes as subjects. His first sculpture of a leading sportsman, in 1984, was Babe Ruth; it now stands in the National Baseball Museum and Hall of Fame in Cooperstown, New York. Shortly afterwards he was commissioned by co-owner of the Boston Red Sox, Jean Yawkey, to sculpt Ted Williams. When unveiled in 1985, the figure moved Williams to tears.

LaMontagne has been doing three-dimensional portraits for over thirty years. Early pieces were more akin to folk art figures, though the elements of realism were starting to appear even then, with carved veins and wrinkles.

Material factors

He later took an interest in carving Native Americans. 'An American Indian would have understood a wood sculpture or could have empathised with it more than marble,' says LaMontagne, adding that there is a warmth to wood that is lacking in other materials. 'I have an affinity with wood because I loved to work it as a youngster. That's why I'm a sculptor who happens to work in wood.'

The first recognised American sculptor, William Rush, carved wood, not stone and, says LaMontagne, 'Wood is more fundamentally American than European, because we have lots of it.'

> ## I do a portrait with a straitjacket on. I just don't have the flexibility. I'm doing a superstar with a superego

Looking further back into history he points out that ancient Egyptian mummy cases were painted and carved, and claims that 'the first wood sculptor who did portraits was an ancient Egyptian'. Now, however, with kiln-dried wood and modern gluing techniques, the wood sculptor has a sturdier, longer-lasting product. If the wood is well protected and kept indoors it should last indefinitely.

Research assistance

Before starting a sculpture, LaMontagne's research is painstaking. Photographs of the subject are taken; extensive measurements of the anatomy are recorded (for Larry Bird's statue he even traced the athlete's hands); the

Babe Ruth, 1984,
LaMontagne's first
sculpture of a sportsman

clothing must be at hand. And to complete the file he paints a life-size portrait that becomes a constant visual reference in his studio.

For Babe Ruth, he complains that he had only black and white photographs and newsreel film to work from. 'You never have enough good photographs of someone deceased,' he laments. When it came to baseball stars Ted Williams and Carl Yastrzemski, although they were alive they had both been years out of uniform and were decades beyond their prime. LaMontagne's solution was to put them into what he calls a time machine and take them back in years. He visualises how the person looked in the past, and

Sculpture is like baseball: it's not something you can learn at Harvard, and your father can't buy it for you. You have to start young and just keep doing it

knowing that bone structure doesn't change, he reverses the ageing process. If he had to, he could put his time machine on fast forward and carve a person as they would look decades from now.

For example, when working on the Ted Williams statue, the sculptor had to work from the features and anatomy of a Ted Williams in his late sixties. Then, with the aid of accumulated photos, he brought the figure back thirty years to his peak at about 35.

'I do a portrait with a straitjacket on,' says LaMontagne. 'I just don't have the flexibility. I'm doing a superstar with a superego who is very much concerned with how he looks. And he is not looking for interpretation....But I'm trying to get not only an accurate portrayal but also some spirit, some presence of mind into the sculpture of what that person is thinking.' He goes so far as to say that he becomes that person.

Capturing the spirit
Certainly LaMontagne's sculptures go beyond just having the right colours and the right shape. Each figure expresses a strong sense of emotion and intensity. For Larry Bird the look had to do with concentration when shooting the foul shot. 'I tried to show a look on his face when nothing else mattered but making the basket.... The moment he is making that shot is one of life and death.'

In the Yastrzemski sculpture the intensity comes from a pose that has him following through on the swung baseball bat. LaMontagne says that he tried to capture 'a feeling of great satis-

faction in the face, that he had already done the deed. It's a serious euphoria, if that's possible. And it happens in an instant. I tried to get that feeling with body motion and facial expression in a split second.'

LaMontagne brings to his sculptures a work ethic that would make his athlete heroes envious. 'Nothing succeeds like excess,' he claims. 'I look to accomplish my goal faster and better. The job at hand must become an obsession. I want to see something done in three months, not six months.... Speed itself is not what I'm after: it's accuracy. But if you're good at what you do, speed is an indication that you know what you're doing.'

Experimental methods
When it comes to tools, LaMontagne goes to extremes: 'There is not a tool made that is big enough for me; there is not a tool made that is small enough for me,' he says. Consequently he is not bound by traditional sculptor's tools and methods. He would use a giant bandsaw to remove wood if he could manipulate a machine big enough to accept the leviathan blocks he works with. Instead, he makes do with a 14in chainsaw, which takes away rectangular blocks of waste wood that can weigh as much as 150lbs, 70kg. After only a week of cutting, a geometric shape begins to emerge.

LaMontagne never carves his figures the same way; faced with a similar problem he may try two very different solutions. He may create the footwear early on for one sculpture and wait until last with another. But whatever the strategy, rounding the wood must be done early on, and this is achieved with large mallets and chisels. Then more exacting definition is given to anatomy, clothing and exposed flesh.

When refining the face, LaMontagne does not use a mallet or heavy gouge; instead he skims the wood, removing very small slivers as he pushes the gouges with his hands. An exacting procedure, he describes it as surgery.

Tricks of the trade
Finally he tackles the fine details. He describes himself as a magician, able to transform wood into nearly any other material. It is a challenge, he says, to take one of nature's raw materials and turn it into fine art.

To make pores, for example, he uses a blunted ice pick to poke at the wood. Shallow skin creases are pressed into the wood with the rounded side of the same tool. For a knitted pattern, he takes a piece of steel, grinds the end into the

Left **Ted Williams, hitter for the Boston Red Sox. The bat is basswood, but looks just like a real ash one**
Right **Life-size sculpture of basketball star Larry Bird, 1987, carved from a single block of laminated basswood**

reverse pattern, and uses the metal as a stamp.

A trademark of LaMontagne's sculptures is the eyes, which not only have depth but also look moist. After painting the details of iris and pupil on the primed surface, he applies as many as twenty coats of glossy polyurethane. The build up of this varnish gives the wet appearance and makes the carvings look as if they are about to blink.

The intensity of the moment is captured in his facial expression

Although it has been said that he sculpts wood as if it were clay, the technique is quite different: his work entails removing material, not adding to it. Unlike clay, wood is not so easy to replace. In fact, LaMontagne is so adept at removing wood that he does not admit to making mistakes. He remembers an art school professor who visited him when he was working on Larry Bird. The man was impressed but felt that this kind of detailed work must have had its share of imperfections. He asked what kind of wood filler he used. LaMontagne was insulted and asked him to leave.

Learning by experience

LaMontagne himself never went to art school, which he says would have been a mistake. 'The trouble with art schools is that everyone uses the same techniques as the teacher. I think art is an individual thing.' He believes in learning the hard way: 'My advice to young people interested in sculpture is to go out and make a bunch of mistakes. Make a big pile of chips and you'll know more than you know now.'

Sculpture is, he believes, like baseball. In Ted Williams' words: 'It's not something you can learn at Harvard, and your father can't buy it for you. You have to start young and just keep doing it.'

Speed itself is not what I'm after: it's accuracy. But if you're good at what you do, speed is an indication that you know what you're doing

The closest LaMontagne got to formal art training was a study grant that took him to Florence, Italy. For a year he studied marble sculpture. During his stay he learned two important lessons: one was that he preferred wood; the other was that even Michelangelo had occasional failures. What people called the artist's unfinished works were to LaMontagne his mistakes.

However, Michelangelo's works and words left a lasting impression on him. He often quotes the Florentine master as saying: 'It takes many trifles to make a masterpiece, but a masterpiece is no trifle.'

LaMontagne continues: 'I believe that what Michelangelo was saying was that it takes a great deal of hard work before you get to the ultimate goal. The steps may not be much but they can add up to something great.' ■

Bobby Orr, former player for the Boston Bruins ice hockey team

Marionettes awaiting their cue. Each head is carved to convey emotion and character

SALZBURG
MARIONETTES
DERICK McGROARTY

A prima donna reduced in stature

The costumes are almost as lavish as a full scale opera

A visit to the Marionettentheater in Salzburg is a treat for carvers and opera lovers.

The Salzburg Marionettes are not the usual kind of puppet theatre. Eighty years ago Anton Aicher carved his wooden heads for personal pleasure before founding a permanent marionette theatre for the presentation of full length operas.

The sculpting of marionette heads is a sophisticated business, that the appearance shows the character is as important as expression and movement. Many early carvings are displayed in the foyer of the theatre, but the present day 'working' marionettes are smaller, about 2' in height, with additional dexterity of facial expression. The progress of the theatre to international

Courtiers of the Pharaoh

status started by Anton's son Herman is now continued in the third generation; the present director Gretl Aicher is the granddaughter of the founder.

Whilst the sumptuous costumes and familiar music are important, the quality and detail of the head sculpting plays a major part in bringing an opera to life.

The main objective of the Marionettentheater is the simple yet artistic presentation of opera. It has succeeded in many countries. The Marionetten performed at the Alexandra Theatre, Birmingham, in March and April 1993. It was an opportunity to see woodcarving contributing to the enjoyment of a wider public audience. ∎

UPPER ROOM

On a visit to Durham, Roger Whiting discovered the ingenious work of Colin Wilbourn

The Upper Room
devised and carved
by Colin Wilbourn,
photograph by
Andy Williams

This article was the last one written by Dr Roger Whiting, who died six weeks after completing it. We are indebted to Joan Whiting-Moon for allowing us to use it.

From a distance the sculpture appears to be a jumble of carved tree trunks

Sculpture has become an attraction in Durham, within the cathedral precincts and along the banks of the River Wear (Wear in this case rhymes with beer). A few yards from Prebends' Bridge is a somewhat puzzling group of thirteen elm trees, whose purpose is not clear unless you know the secret.

As you walk round them you will realise that the carvings on twelve of the tree trunks are related in some way. The penny will drop as you sit in the seat carved in the thirteenth trunk. From the seat the carvings on the twelve trees fit together, into a relief carving of the upper room of the last supper.

Viewed from anywhere else the carving is confused and the perspective distorted.

This impressive display of two and three-dimensional art was made by Colin Wilbourn, during his time as Artist-in-Residence at Durham Cathedral in 1986-87. Colin was the first sculptor to be appointed to the post. While he was there he heard that thirteen elm trees belonging to the Dean and Chapter of Durham had died of Dutch elm disease and were to be felled. He suggested that the tree trunks should be used to create a sculpture.

Concept

The idea of creating the Upper Room was a progression from the piece he was working on when he heard about the elm trees – the *Last Supper Table*. The *Upper Room* allowed Colin to make a sculpture specific to a particular place, physically and spiritually. Physically the trees were not far from where they had grown. Spiritually, not only was the subject appropriate to the cathedral grounds, but there were thirteen trees for the thirteen at the last supper.

One aim of the sculpture was to totally involve just one person at a time – letting them see what others could not – by making the sculpture only complete for the person seated in the thirteenth tree,

Colin restricted access to that view. Part of the piece is an attempt to point out that people see the world from different viewpoints, so they will have different appreciations of things. As the viewer completes the sculpture by sitting in the seat they become part of the creation process themselves – they cannot 'create' the sculpture unless they sit in the seat. People

become actively involved in the piece rather than just passively gazing at it.

Much of the credit for this spectacular sculpture must go to Northern Arts, as they provided the additional finance necessary for the completion of the work, which was started towards the end of Colin's residency.

Construction

Colin began work while the trees were lying felled on the ground. He measured them and drew their shapes so that he could make scale models of them in card. The cardboard cutout trees were used to plan where the trees would be planted in relation to each other and the seat. A full-sized ground plan was drawn, before the holes were dug and twelve of the tree trunks were erected. The thirteenth, the seat, was not positioned, as Colin needed to place his 'perspectograph' on the viewpoint.

The perspectograph was made in three operations. First a pole with a spy-hole on the top was positioned on the viewpoint - this would not be moved until all the carving was complete. A sheet of clear plastic was supported in a frame in front of the tree trunks, and looking through the spy-hole the outline of the trees was drawn on the plastic. The plastic with the precise outline was taken back to the studio and a drawing of the intended carving was carefully positioned on the outline of the trees.

Colin Wilbourn and the elm trees ready for the chainsaw

The view through the wire drawing, used to transfer the flat perspective on to the trees

The key to the Upper Room

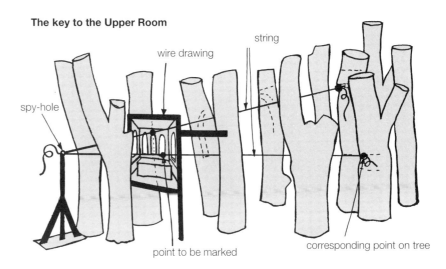

spy-hole

wire drawing

string

point to be marked

corresponding point on tree

**Set up for carving, the
spy-hole on the left, the
wire drawing in position**

From this a wire 'drawing' of the architecture of the room was made, with the perspective correct for the one viewpoint.

The wire drawing was the key to making the carving work properly. With the wire drawing fixed in the frame, string tied to the spy-hole was held in tension through the wire drawing and on to the trees. In this ingenious way the key points of the room were marked, preserving the perspective view.

Cutting started with an 18in, 460mm Stihl chainsaw. When the trees had been prepared, finer work was done using chisels and gouges, with a heavy mallet made from an old lignum

vitae bowling ball.

This combination of large scale work and a heavy mallet led to the destruction of numerous tool handles. Colin has a collection of about forty carving tools, a mixture of Henry Taylor, Ashley Iles and Pfeil with some older makes.

The seat is comparatively simple, in relation to the rest of the *Upper Room*, but its position is critical.

The *Upper Room* is a drawing carved on to a 'canvas' of twelve separate objects. The concept is remarkable and the execution a display of craftsmanship and ingenuity. Colin Wilbourn has created a truly marvellous piece of work in the *Upper Room*. ■

INDEX